Deterrence
in the
Second Nuclear Age

Deterrence
in the
Second Nuclear Age

Keith B. Payne

The University Press of Kentucky

Copyright © 1996 by The University Press of Kentucky

Scholarly publisher for the Commonwealth, serving
Bellarmine College, Berea College, Centre College of
Kentucky, Eastern Kentucky University, The Filson Club,
Georgetown College, Kentucky Historical Society,
Kentucky State University, Morehead State University,
Murray State University, Northern Kentucky University,
Transylvania University, University of Kentucky,
University of Louisville, and Western Kentucky University.

Editorial and Sales Offices: The University Press of Kentucky
663 South Limestone Street, Lexington, Kentucky, 40508-4008

00 99 98 97 96   5 4 3 2 1

Library of Congress Cataloging-in-Publication Data

Payne, Keith B.
      Deterrence in the second nuclear age / Keith B. Payne.
            p.   cm.
      Includes bibliographical references and index.
      ISBN 0-8131-1998-7 (cloth : alk. paper). — ISBN 0-8131-0895-0
      (paper : alk. paper)
      1. United States—Military policy. 2. Deterrence (Strategy)
      3. World politics—1989-   . I. Title
      UA23.P3747   1996
      327.1'7—dc20   96-30435

This book is printed on acid-free recycled paper meeting the
requirements of the American National Standard for
Permanence of Paper for Printed Library Materials.

Manufactured in the United States of America

For little Sarah,

full of joy

Contents

Foreword

Why did the great Cold War not conclude with a nuclear World War III? Were we clever, or lucky, or both? Did our policies of nuclear deterrence prevent a war that otherwise would have occurred? In *Deterrence in the Second Nuclear Age*, Keith Payne sets out neither to praise deterrence nor to bury it. Indeed in a major achievement he has administered a distinctly nonroutine examination of deterrence, without killing the patient.

All too rarely, genuinely important books appear on the broad subject of national and international security. This book is one such. I invite anyone skeptical of the promise of novelty concerning the theory and practice of deterrence to put their skepticism aside and give this study a chance. In a carefully nuanced assessment, Payne argues that the general theory of deterrence is attractive but that general theory always requires translation for local conditions. We may be masters of deterrence theory, but do we know—really know with any appreciable confidence—how to deter the leaders of a particular government, on particular issues, at a particular time? The answer here is a cautionary "not likely."

Unfortunately, many current and past policymakers have not understood this caveat. Keith Payne reminds us that deterrence is a relational variable; a would-be foe has to choose to be deterred. And, most important, the United States by its word and deed cannot control that choice.

This book advises sensibly that whatever deterrence can accomplish it should be allowed to accomplish. Yet there are significant limits to the practicable scope for, and efficacy of, a strategy of deterrence. Payne shows, on the one hand, truly how "rough and ready" our possible success with deterrence in the Cold War may have been (again, were we lucky?), and how much more strenuous still are the tests for deterrence likely to be in the future.

Here, in one concise text, is a readable, constructive, empathic critique of past deterrence theory and would-be practice that both highlights what needs saving from nearly half a century of scholarship and policy, and exposes relentlessly our persisting errors in logic and frailties in behavior, the consequences of which can be fatal. Readers will not find herein any stale replay of yesterday's debates. The argument of the book is rooted firmly in history, but is both forward looking in purpose and nonpolemical in style. Payne does not conceal his distaste for the concept and practice of Assured Vulnerability, but the edge of his argument cuts away at error on all sides of defense debate. He exposes the fallacies in the widespread expectation that deterrence can be made reliable and predictable—an expectation that reflects a fundamental confusion about the subject, but nevertheless is held across the political spectrum.

Deterrence in the Second Nuclear Age is, in a very real sense, quite a shocking book. Many readers will discover that Payne's moderate and balanced prose contains a near heretical but also inescapable message. Specifically, the U.S. government, and the host of "experts" who advise it, actually *know* a great deal less about the practicability of deterrence (which is to say about war, peace, and survival) than they think they know. Payne does not allege that these people are deliberately advancing lethal falsehoods. The situation in reality is more dangerous than that. There is peril in the misplaced self-confidence of officials and advisers who believe they know how to deter. Their resultant bravado should frighten us all.

Keith Payne's tour de force has been many years in gestation. This is a mature book that should influence noticeably both the course of scholarship and—dare one be so optimistic?—the path of public policy and national security strategy. This is a book that can make a difference to our security.

Colin S. Gray
Professor of International Politics and
Director of the Centre for Security Studies
University of Hull, England

Preface

No one had time for a deliberate aim or time to think. . . . There is no mystery about the outbreak of the First World War. The deterrent failed to deter. This was to be expected sooner or later. A deterrent may work ninety-nine times out of a hundred. On the hundredth occasion it produces catastrophe. There is a contemporary moral here for those who like to find one.

—A.J.P. Taylor, *War By Timetable*

The focus of this book is on deterrence. During the Cold War deterrence of the Soviet Union was the leitmotiv of U.S. and NATO military strategy. In the United States the question of how best to deter the Soviet Union was at the heart of the debate about nuclear weapons and most other controversies concerning arms control agreements and specific strategic weapons programs.

The rancorous debates about the MX ICBM, the Strategic Defense Initiative (popularly known as "Star Wars"), the nuclear "freeze" initiatives of the early 1970s and early 1980s, and the SALT II agreement, for example, generally reflected underlying differences over the requirements for deterrence. These highly visible controversies that seemed to revolve around technical-sounding issues and considerations truly represented only the tip of an iceberg; the larger underlying issue was how to deter the Soviet Union.

The question of how to deter will be as important in the post–Cold War era as it was during the Cold War. Yet, as the 1991 war with Iraq foreshadowed, the question of how to deter will increasingly have to be broadened to include so-called regional rogue powers. The convenience of focusing largely on a single adversary in this regard is over.

This by no means is to suggest an expectation that the Russian Federation is likely to be an insignificant or necessarily benign player on the post–Cold War world stage. Rather, additional states are acquiring the instruments of power to compel the broadening of our scope concerning the question of how to deter. In particular, the proliferation of weapons of mass destruction

(WMD) and advanced missile systems is causing us to take increasing notice of regional powers—powers that in the past may have been of interest primarily or solely for the role they might have played in the great East-West contest.

Some rogue states, for example, seek WMD in part to establish a free hand for themselves in their respective areas of interest—free, that is, from the prospective limitations otherwise that might be imposed by Western interests and, more to the point, Western superiority in conventional military technology. How might we deter these emerging regional powers armed with WMD? And how different will the answer to that question be from the vintage Cold War answers? These questions will be of unprecedented interest for coming years.

There are many other important post–Cold War security issues, such as how to prevent proliferation. The focus of this book, however, is not on the admittedly important question of nonproliferation; there are numerous recent treatments of the question, and in any event the question of how to deter "rogues" armed with WMD will require our attention whatever our nonproliferation efforts and successes: some countries will see great value in WMD and their means of delivery and persevere until they have acquired them. The question of how to deter such countries may only pique our interest now but it will become paramount in the future.

In fact, some of those countries now most vocal in their self-identified hostility to the United States also appear to be those most intent on acquiring missiles and WMD: Iran, Libya, and North Korea, for example. And we continue to be surprised by UN reports on Iraqi efforts in this regard. The acquisition of WMD by such rogues is a reasonable cause for concern and will be difficult to prevent, in some cases probably impossible.

Consequently, the focus here is on how to deter in the post–Cold War era, when "doomsday weapons will be in the hands of many," and to explore whether Cold War answers may usefully guide us. What will the differences of the post–Cold War context mean for the reliability and effectiveness of deterrence policy? These questions and their answers will shape U.S. strategy and forces for years to come.

Acknowledgments

I am thankful for the friends, colleagues, and family who contributed directly or indirectly to this book. Without their contributions it would not have been completed. My wife, Beth, not only provided necessary moral support, but also suffered through proofreading the first draft of the manuscript with good humor. Professor Colin Gray, Lieutenant General William Odom, U.S. Army (Ret.), Kurt Guthe, and Dr. Michael Altfeld reviewed the entire manuscript at various stages; each provided very useful suggestions for its revision. At different stages of the Cold War Professor Gray and the late Herman Kahn were at the intellectual forefront of thinking about deterrence theory and its application. Together, almost two decades ago, they set me on the course of examining that theory against the historical record; I am very grateful for both that guidance and the continuing education they provided me. Several colleagues at the National Institute for Public Policy helped in the never-ending search for the proper historical references and factual tidbits, including Willis Stanley, Bernard Victory, and Karma Whaley. Amy Moltaji produced the final manuscript, and its numerous predecessors, with her usual great skill and good-natured patience.

My children have taught me much about the limited practicability of deterrence theory; my appreciation of the need to prepare for deterrence failure was sharpened when the older gingerly plucked her little sister from the deep end of a swimming pool, after one of my attempts at deterrence failed.

Finally, in completing this book I have drawn lightly from several of my previously published works and appreciate the permission to do so granted by the publishers of the following articles and book chapters: "Deterring Weapons of Mass Destruction: Lessons from History," in *Confronting Weapons of Mass Destruction: Challenges for U.S. Planning*, ed. Stuart E. Johnson (Washington, D.C.: National Defense University Press, 1996); "Post-Cold War Deterrence and Missile Defense," *Orbis* 39, no. 2 (spring 1995); "Proliferation, Deterrence, Stability and Missile Defense," *Comparative Strategy* 13, no. 1 (January–March 1994); "Deterrence and U.S. Strategic Force Requirements After the Cold War,"

Comparative Strategy 11, no. 3 (July–September 1992); "Munich: Fifty Years After," in *The Meaning of Munich: Fifty Years Later*, ed. Kenneth Jensen and David Wurmser (Washington, D.C.: U.S. Institute of Peace, 1990); and, (with Lawrence Fink) "Deterrence without Defense: Gambling on Perfection," *Strategic Review* 16, no. 1 (Winter 1989).

Abbreviations

ABM	antiballistic missile
ACDA	Arms Control and Disarmament Agency
ASD	assistant secretary of defense
BMD	ballistic missile defense
DPRK	Democratic People's Republic of Korea
FBIS-CHI	Foreign Broadcast Information Service—China
FBIS-EAS	Foreign Broadcast Information Service—East Asia
FBIS-NES	Foreign Broadcast Information Service—Near East & South Asia
FBIS-UMA	Foreign Broadcast Information Service—Central Eurasia Military Affairs
GPO	U.S. Government Printing Office
ICBM	intercontinental ballistic missile
MAD	mutual assured destruction
MX	missile experimental
NMD	national missile defense
NPT	Nuclear Nonproliferation Treaty
NSC	National Security Council
OTA	Office of Technology Assessment
PD	presidential directive
(P)DUSD	principal deputy undersecretary of defense
SALT	Strategic Arms Limitation Talks
SDI	Strategic Defense Initiative
START	Strategic Arms Reduction Talks
TMD	theater missile defense
UNSCOM	United Nations Special Commission for the Disarmament of Iraq
WEU	Western European Union
WMD	weapons of mass destruction

Chapter 1
Introduction

To win one hundred victories in one hundred battles is not the acme of skill. To subdue the enemy without fighting is the acme of skill.

—Sun Tzu, sixth century, B.C.

The word deterrence may bring to mind the Cold War's "balance of terror" and threats of nuclear "mutual assured destruction." During the Cold War, U.S. policies of deterrence vis-à-vis the Soviet Union focused on nuclear weapons and nuclear threats. These deterrence policies and the nuclear weapons supporting them became the focus of an often noisy and cantankerous public debate concerning U.S.-Soviet relations and nuclear weapons.

The debate about nuclear weapons in the United States often descended to "bumper-sticker" sloganeering, supposedly pitting thoughtful anti-nuclear activists against a primitive and malevolent military-industrial complex. That characterization of the nuclear debate, popularized in much commentary on the subject, may have been useful politically, but was a gross distortion.[1] Serious debate about nuclear weapons actually revolved around the question of how to deter the Soviet Union and the related role for nuclear weapons in policies of deterrence.

Thinking about deterrence in "balance of terror" terms probably hinders more than helps understanding. Deterrence should be considered in a much broader context. Although policies of deterrence were in fact central to the rationale for U.S. nuclear weapons during the Cold War, at a more general level deterrence is one of the most important and prevalent modes of behavior between individuals as well as between countries. It is neither new to the nuclear age nor relevant only to military considerations. Indeed, it is a standard feature of familial and community relations.

---

1. A vapid and heavy-handed good versus evil approach masqueraded as thoughtful analysis in many treatments of the subject during the early 1980s. See, for example, Ronald Sider and Richard Taylor, *Nuclear Holocaust and Christian Hope* (Downers Grove, Ill.: InterVarsity, 1982); Robert Scheer, *With Enough Shovels* (New York: Random House, 1982); and Helen Caldicott, *Missile Envy: The Arms Race and Nuclear War*, rev. ed. (New York: Bantam, 1986).

Thinking about deterrence in these more familiar contexts, at least initially, is a useful route to understanding its role in international relations.

All in the Family

Given the association of deterrence with Cold War nuclear issues, it may seem harsh to suggest that it could have anything to do with familial relations. Yet, deterrence clearly is practiced widely among family members. Parents the world over tend to be experienced practitioners of deterrence vis-à-vis their children. There obviously are many significant differences between the parent-child relationship and state-to-state relations, but the basic deterrence mechanism is important in each.

When mothers and fathers try to discourage their children from doing some mischief, they typically warn of the punishment sure to follow any such behavior. If, for example, a youngster who cannot swim well appears to be contemplating a move toward the deep water at the local swimming pool or pond, a sharp parental warning usually comes quickly. Before expending the time and energy necessary to move the youngster physically, parents hope that a stern warning will be sufficient to change the child's course.

If the child understands the warning, considers the risks of continuing on course, and consequently decides to stay put, the parents have practiced deterrence effectively. For parents, deterrence offers real advantages. They are able to shape the child's behavior as desired, with minimum exertion and without open conflict with the child. In addition, instead of reacting after trouble unfolded, they have prevented it from occurring in the first place. (It should be noted that anyone with much experience poolside can attest to the frequent failure of parental deterrence policies.)

At another level, deterrence is a key component in preventing crime. For example, signs at department stores and supermarkets frequently announce that "shoplifters will be prosecuted to the full extent of the law." The store's management, of course, hopes that these warnings will lead a would-be thief to believe that the risks of shoplifting will outweigh the possible gains, and therefore to choose not to shoplift. Such warning signs represent an attempt to deter. Again, effective deterrence is much to be preferred to the alternatives. Rather than reacting to a crime already committed, with the risky, time-consuming, and costly process of actually catching a thief, it is hoped that effective deterrence can prevent the shoplifting from occurring, in this case, at the trivial expense of a warning sign.

In each case, whether parents warn a child or the store management warns potential thieves, the hoped-for result is the same: the person to be deterred comprehends the risks, weighs the potential costs and benefits, judges the potential costs to be greater than the benefits, and therefore decides against the unwanted behavior in question. In principle, the requirements for effective deterrence are not daunting. The person to be deterred must be informed of the threat, believe the threat is at least plausible, and rationally weigh the potential "cost" of the threat against the value of choosing to go ahead with the forbidden action. "Rational" in this sense simply describes a decision-making process in which the person to be deterred is informed of the situation (that is, takes in information), weighs the alternative courses of action as to the pros and cons of their likely outcomes, and chooses that course judged to give the best return according to the person's hierarchy of values.[2] The child rationally chooses to stay away from the deep water because, for the child, whatever pleasure might come from being in the "adult" section of the pool is not worth the subsequent parental displeasure and punishment. For the shoplifter, whatever might be the value of committing the crime, it is not worth the possible consequences. It is important to note that in these hypothetical examples of effective deterrence, the persons attempting to deter—in these cases, parents and store management—must pose a threat that speaks to the respective value hierarchy of the child and the shoplifter, is understood, and is considered at least plausible.

The Advantages of Deterrence

The advantages of an effective policy of deterrence are evident from the examples offered above. Effective deterrence conserves effort on the part of those issuing the warning because no action is

---

2. I have described "procedural rationality" here. For a useful and concise discussion of rationality in deterrence theory, see Alex Hybel, *Power over Rationality* (Albany: State Univ. of New York Press, 1993), 16–19. For an early and still useful discussion of rationality, see Stephen Maxwell, *Rationality in Deterrence*, Adelphi Papers, no. 50 (London: Institute for Strategic Studies, August 1968); see also Frank Zagare, "Rationality and Deterrence," *World Politics* 42, no. 2 (January 1990): 238-60.

necessary to enforce their preferred behavior: the child or thief has changed behavior of his or her own accord before the unwanted action occurs. Because deterrence here is preventive rather than reactive, it typically involves less effort by the parent or store management than would be the case if the situation had to be re-solved by direct action.

Not surprisingly, the immediate advantages of an effective de-terrence policy—obvious in these everyday examples—also make deterrence a highly desirable part of a country's national security strategy. The Department of Defense defines deterrence as "the prevention from action by fear of the consequences. Deterrence is a state of mind brought about by the existence of a credible threat of unacceptable counteraction."[3] If the opponent's "state of mind" can be manipulated so that the opponent decides against attacking or pursuing some provocative course, there may be no need for direct military engagement. That is, if an opponent can be led to act in preferred ways without battle, a country can protect its interests while avoiding the possibly severe risks and costs of battle.

Given this tremendous advantage of a successful deterrence policy, there is little wonder that Sun Tzu, the great Chinese strategist of the sixth century B.C., observed that the ability to de-ter and coerce an opponent is superior even to the ability to defeat an opponent in battle: "For to win one hundred victories in one hundred battles is not the acme of skill. To subdue the enemy without fighting is the acme of skill."[4] Sun Tzu clearly was not a pacifist, and his point is not to dismiss the value of winning battles. His point is that placing an opponent in a position wherein that opponent decides not to challenge or provoke, but instead accepts one's desired course, is far superior to engaging the opponent in battle to enforce one's will. According to Sun Tzu, only when one is unable to deter or coerce without resort to force must one pursue the more risky and costly alternative of doing battle.

Following Sun Tzu's principle, the unparalleled U.S. and allied victory over Iraq in the 1991 Persian Gulf war did not reflect "the acme of skill." The Gulf war certainly represented one of the most

3. *Department of Defense Dictionary of Military and Associated Terms*, Joint Pub. 1-02 (Washington, D.C.: GPO, 23 March 1994), 115.

4. *Sun Tzu: The Art of War*, trans. Samuel B. Griffith (Oxford: Oxford Univ. Press, 1963), 77.

dramatic military victories in history. Nevertheless, deterring Saddam Hussein from invading Kuwait or successfully coercing him to leave Kuwait without battle would have demonstrated the highest level of skill. Of course, neither route might have been feasible in practice.

Deterrence and the Cold War

As Sun Tzu's writings demonstrate, strategists have long understood that the capability to deter is "the acme of skill." With the emergence of the nuclear stalemate during the Cold War, Sun Tzu's admonitions were taken to their logical conclusion. Engaging the opponent without resort to force (that is, deterring and coercing) not only was advantageous in the context of the enormous superpower nuclear arsenals; in many ways it was the only reasonable option available. This point was recognized very early in the nuclear age by the brilliant theorist and military historian Bernard Brodie. Looking forward, Brodie offered the view in 1946 that "thus far the chief purpose of our military establishment has been to win wars. From now on, its chief purpose must be to avert them."[5]

National security strategy is about the use of power of all kinds to achieve national goals; military strategy is about the use of military power in support of national goals. The U.S.-Soviet nuclear stalemate introduced a limit on the extent to which the actual use of military power could support national goals. With nuclear weapons available to both superpowers in such abundance by the late 1960s, there was a limit to the level of conflict and provocation that could serve any political purpose.

Because the United States confronted a Soviet Union easily capable of annihilating the fabric of U.S. society with nuclear weapons, U.S. freedom to engage the Soviet Union militarily was limited. Under the conditions of such utter societal vulnerability to the opponent, the use of extreme force against the opponent in support of a national goal was not an option consistent with national survival. A provocation expected to lead to direct hostilities, and the likelihood of large-scale nuclear war, could be considered only under the direst of circumstances.

---

5. Bernard Brodie, "Implications for Military Policy," in Brodie, ed., *The Absolute Weapon* (New York: Harcourt Brace, 1946), 76.

Thus during the Cold War, the actual use of force leading to a general nuclear war became disconnected from any possible national goal. A superpower nuclear conflict could, according to some estimates of extreme circumstances, have led to some 160 million U.S. dead.[6] No use of force that culminated in the destruction of the nation could be related reasonably to support for achieving national goals. Nuclear weapons had uprooted traditional notions of military strategy: their use could not contribute to anything worthy of the name "victory" because no national goal could be worth the cost of general nuclear war. This situation logically led to the development of limited and proxy war theories by "the best and the brightest" during the Kennedy and Johnson administrations. It also led to the ascendancy of deterrence in U.S. military strategy vis-à-vis the Soviet Union. In relations with the Soviet Union, the actual employment of nuclear weapons had become disconnected from supporting national objectives, but the *threat* of their use became central to military strategy. Persuading the Soviet leadership that our nuclear threats were credible in this context came to be of paramount concern.

The focus of traditional military strategy was to prevent an enemy from achieving its military objectives and to attain one's own by defeating the enemy's military establishment; on occasion deterrent effect could be found in the capability to do so. In contrast, nuclear deterrence policy attempted to shape an enemy's behavior by threatening its homeland with nuclear attack, without the prior requirement of defeating its military establishment.

Because deterrence gained ascendancy in U.S. military strategy vis-à-vis the Soviet Union, the key question became how to deter. What Soviet actions should the U.S. attempt to deter by nuclear threat? What should be the character of the nuclear threat behind the U.S. deterrence policy? What types of forces were helpful or unhelpful for deterrence? To whom and how should nuclear threats be communicated? How could those threats be made believable to the Soviet leadership? These became the critical questions. The answers were not obvious.

---

6. Estimates of nuclear war casualties became a highly debated and contentious issue as deterrence policies involving the threat of limited nuclear use gained visibility. The fatality level cited here is from U.S. Congress, Office of Technology Assessment, *The Effects of Nuclear War* (Washington, D.C., OTA, May 1979), 8.

Learning How To Deter

In the illustrations given of familial and community deterrence, answers to the basic questions about how to deter are also not obvious. In such cases, however, there are many opportunities for testing various approaches to deterrence to determine which approach works best. If deterrence fails several or many times, the result need not be disastrous: the parent can spring to action if the toddler does not heed the warning about going too near the pool; the store detective can pursue the shoplifter if necessary.

In contrast, during the Cold War the U.S. could not road test various approaches to deterrence policy vis-à-vis the Soviet Union to determine which policy worked best. The occasions for testing nuclear deterrence policies were too few and unpredictable, and our information about the opponent's decision-making too limited, to allow an understanding of why deterrence might have worked or failed. The penalty for failure was too high to engage in a conscious testing scheme.[7]

Consequently, a debate about how best to deter the Soviet Union and what forces were necessary for deterrence raged throughout the Cold War. The basic issues in this debate changed very little over the years: in the 1970s and 1980s it pitted the so-called nuclear war-fighting approach to deterrence against the mutual assured destruction (MAD) approach.[8] The labels occasionally changed, but the basic differences upon which positions were based did not. The debate about U.S. nuclear weapons, when not carried on at a bumper-sticker level of sloganeering, reflected this deeper debate about how to deter. Finding the truth, in any scientific sense, simply was impossible because there was insufficient evidence to demonstrate the superiority of one approach to deterrence over another. On this base of ignorance, competing assertions about how best to deter and what level of weaponry was necessary for deterrence could simply be repeated with vigor, without much apparent risk of being demonstrably wrong.

---

7. In many discussions of deterrence theory with the late Herman Kahn, one of the foremost pioneers in the field, he mused that the testing of various approaches to nuclear deterrence would require at least one hundred test cases, including cases in which deterrence failed; clearly such testing would be infeasible.

8. These alternative approaches to U.S. strategic deterrence policy are discussed in detail in Chapter 3, with an emphasis on their similarities.

Consequently, during the early-to-mid 1980s, advocates of a freeze in nuclear capabilities could argue that ceasing any further development of nuclear weapons would help stabilize the U.S.-Soviet deterrence balance.[9] In contrast, noted strategic commentators could argue simultaneously that proper nuclear modernization (that is, continued development and deployment of some U.S. nuclear forces) was necessary to help stabilize the deterrence balance.[10] A nuclear freeze became the rallying cry of the political left and the arms control community, while the need for continued modernization was the refrain of conservative skeptics of a freeze.

Which side in this nuclear debate was correct? Would a nuclear freeze or nuclear modernization contribute more to deterrence stability? Despite the strength with which these contrasting positions were presented, there was, in fact, little basis for demonstrating which view was more or less valid. Both views could not have been valid, but neither could be demonstrated conclusively wrongheaded. Consequently, the debate could continue without resolution, driven largely by personalities and politics. With so little basis for demonstrating error, the debate about deterrence and nuclear weapons could reflect whatever view was most fashionable at the time, most compatible with public opinion, most salable to Congress, most in line with arms control deal-making or defense budget pressures, or myriad other secondary factors. Competing assertions were simply repeated with great gusto until the debate tired and political fashion moved to other issues. In fact, the debate subsided only because the collapse of the Soviet Union rendered it seemingly moot.

Old Questions and a New Nuclear Age

Questions about deterrence, however, are presenting themselves anew as we leave the Cold War behind and enter the second nuclear age. This label, the "second nuclear age" was originated by Colin Gray of the University of Hull, and seems quite helpful to thinking about the subject. It suggests that so many features of the

---

9. See the testimony of Randall Forsberg in U.S. House, Committee on Foreign Relations, *The Role of Arms Control in U.S. Defense Policy: Hearing before the Committee on Foreign Relations*, 98th Cong., 2d sess. (Washington, D.C.: GPO, 1984), 112.

10. See the testimony of R. James Woolsey in ibid., 114.

emerging security environment are sufficiently different from that of the Cold War that the post–Cold War period deserves to be considered a new, yet still nuclear, age.[11] The dominant features of this second nuclear age began to emerge by the end of the 1980s and became clearer by the end of 1991, with the collapse of the Soviet Union and the overwhelming victory over Iraq by the U.S. and its allied coalition in the Gulf war. On the benign side of the ledger, the Warsaw Pact and the Soviet Union collapsed, ending the dangerous bloc-to-bloc confrontation in Europe that involved the world's largest concentration of opposing military forces. Germany was reunited, ending the tense standoff on the intra-German border. The leaders of the Soviet Union and subsequently the Russian Federation appeared to have decided upon a more cooperative course of relations with the West—essentially agreeing for the first time to serious arms reductions and cooperating diplomatically with the Coalition's war effort against Iraq, a former Soviet ally.

The second nuclear age, however, also features some disturbing trends. First, regional powers, no longer participants in the discipline of the old bloc-to-bloc confrontation, appear to be at greater liberty to pursue local animosities and grievances, leading to local crises that in some cases challenge U.S. interests.[12]

Second, the proliferation of weapons of mass destruction,[13] advanced conventional weapons, and modern means of delivery (for example, ballistic and cruise missiles) appear to be promising otherwise third-rate military powers access to weapons of unprecedented lethality. These powers generally may not soon be able to achieve high accuracies for WMD, or integrate WMD into their existing military establishments so as to provide a systematic "combined arms" war-fighting capability. They will, nevertheless, acquire the WMD and delivery means necessary to pose

---

11. For an excellent assessment of the alternative national security strategies potentially available to the United States, and a recommended course for the United States in this second nuclear age, see William Odom, *America's Military Revolution* (Washington, D.C.: American Univ. Press, 1993).

12. As Edward Luttwak observes in this regard, "Now that the Cold War no longer suppresses hot wars, the entire culture of disciplined restraint in the use of force is in dissolution." See "Toward Post-Heroic Warfare," *Foreign Affairs* 74, no. 3 (May-June 1995): 109–22.

13. WMD typically are thought to include chemical, biological, nuclear, and radiological weapons. For an outstanding assessment of the threat posed by the proliferation of WMD, see Kathleen Bailey, *Doomsday Weapons in the Hands of Many* (Urbana: Univ. of Illinois Press, 1991).

unprecedented threats to urban areas; that is, WMD will at least provide them with tools for deterrence and coercion. The pace of proliferation may be debated, but the direction and trends are now obvious: toward the greater diffusion of WMD and delivery means of longer-range, greater payload, and better accuracy.[14] Rather than focusing so intently on U.S.-Russian relations, questions about deterrence now typically concern how to deter regional powers newly armed with WMD. Although the players have changed, the same questions about deterrence that were left unresolved from the Cold War debate remain. Can we deter opponents whom we would prefer not to have to engage in battle, and if so, how?

At this point, it may be useful to come back to the distinction between the examples of deterrence from family life and those from international relations. In family relations the question of "what deters" can be tested and different approaches practiced on many occasions over the course of months and years. The hope, of course, is that effective parenting practices can be learned and that the learning process will not be too frustrating or unhappy for either parent or child. Much of the literature aimed at parents involves advice about the possible methods of shaping a young child's behavior, including through deterrence (although this term is not used). Through trial and error, and with many occasions to observe what seems best in shaping their child's actions, parents hope to understand how to deter unwanted behavior. Child development specialists base their advice on numerous observations that can support general principles—principles that will be helpful for most children most of the time.

In the sphere of international conflict, the testing of possible answers to the question of "what deters" is not so easy. The occasions for testing a particular approach to deterrence may be few and far between. And those potential occasions for testing deterrence that do arise may involve far different conditions—different challenges by different leaders, with different stakes, and different types of provocation to be deterred. Even if deterrence can be shown to have worked in one case, it's not clear that many specific lessons can be learned that will be useful for the next occasion. In fact, knowing whether and when a policy of deterrence has

---

14. For a thoughtful discussion of this proposition by an international group of experts, see Kathleen Bailey and Robert Rudney, eds., *Proliferation and Export Controls* (Lanham, Md.: Univ. Press of America, 1993).

"worked" may be difficult because there may be little evidence available of its success. Leaders may understandably be reluctant to publicize when they have been restrained from a provocation by an opponent's deterrent threat. Why help an opponent with the information necessary to establish an effective policy of deterrence? Would it not be better to misinform an opponent on such matters?

Consequently, policies of deterrence may be or appear to be effective dozens of times, without a trace of evidence on which to base general or specific lessons. Similarly, when a deterrence policy obviously fails, the parties involved may not be anxious to publicize the decision-making that could explain why it failed. Perhaps most obvious, international crises are not the optimal occasions for a leadership to engage in the road testing of deterrence policies. The price of deterrence failure may be so high in a military crisis that the idea of purposely testing or "trying out" a particular approach to deterrence would be absurd. Finally, even when a crisis has occurred, and evidence is available concerning how and why leaders behaved as they did, different interpretations of events and questions about underlying motives are virtually certain. And even when information is available, establishing a confident basis for specific lessons about deterrence for the future may be very difficult.

In short, while parents may, through long and sometimes rocky experience, learn how to shape their children's behavior, learning "how to deter" in the international context is much more difficult. Lessons learned in the past—beyond providing the possible base for some very general principles—may be irrelevant if the next set of conditions surrounding a crisis varies in significant respects from the previous experience.

Deterrence in the Second Nuclear Age

The question of whether Cold War approaches to deterrence will, in fact, work in the second nuclear age, including against "rogue" regional powers such as Iraq, Iran, North Korea, China, and Libya, is becoming increasingly critical for several reasons. First, it has become obvious that regional conflicts are a prominent feature of the second nuclear age, including conflicts that may challenge U.S. interests. Recent history has seen the projection of U.S. military power to Panama, Iraq, Somalia, Haiti, Macedonia, and Bosnia, and a 1994 crisis with North Korea over the issue of nuclear arms that reportedly nearly led to U.S. military action.[15] If, as appears likely in these early years of the second nuclear age, we can anticipate increasing challenges from regional powers and a continuing felt need to counter those challenges, we must soon determine whether now-traditional Cold War approaches to U.S. deterrence policy can be applied usefully to so-called rogue states and regional challengers.

In addition to the apparent increase in potential regional crises, proliferation—a defining feature of the second nuclear age—is compelling us to consider anew "how to deter." The global proliferation of WMD and advanced delivery capabilities is a widely acknowledged trend. Although it is difficult to identify the full scope of the proliferation problem, the following is illustrative:

- At present, at least fifteen countries have an offensive chemical weapon program and at least ten countries have an offensive biological weapon program.[16]

- By the end of the 1990s, twenty or more developing countries could acquire missiles either overtly or covertly.[17]

- At least ten countries reportedly are interested in nuclear weapons development.[18]

---

15. Some of the apparent increase in regional instability appears, at least in part, to be a result of the ending of the Cold War and the erosion of bloc discipline. It appears, for example, that the collapse of the Soviet Union was one of the factors motivating Saddam Hussein—on the assumption that the Soviet collapse would give the United States a "free hand" in the Middle East and that the United States would, as a result, encourage Israel to embark on "new stupidities." Saddam Hussein, quoted in Don Oberdorfer, "Missed Signals in the Middle East," *Washington Post Magazine*, 17 March 1991, 20, 22.

16. See the prepared statement by Admiral William Studeman, Acting Director of Central Intelligence, in U.S. Senate, Committee on Armed Services, *Worldwide Threat to the United States: Hearing before the Committee on Armed Services*, 104th Cong., 1st sess. (Washington, D.C.: GPO, 1995), 9.

17. As reported in Department of Defense, *Annual Report to the President and the Congress* (Washington D.C.: GPO, February 1992), 65.

18. U.S. Congress, Office of Technology Assessment, *Proliferation of Weapons of Mass Destruction: Assessing the Risks*, OTA-ISC-559 (Washington, D.C.: GPO, August 1993), 64. The countries listed by OTA are the "usual suspects" most often mentioned in connection with an interest in nuclear weapons development; the list is not the official assessment of a

- At least twenty-four countries have chemical weapons programs in various stages of development.[19]

There is a general consensus that the diffusion of the technology and know-how necessary to produce WMD and various means for their delivery, including ballistic and cruise missiles, is an inevitable function of educational, economic, and technological advancement in developing countries. As General Li Jijun, deputy director of the Military Science Institute in Beijing has observed about proliferation, "The information age too will ultimately render even the most developed society open to attack and paralysis."[20]

There is little risk in predicting that in a forthcoming regional crisis, Western political leaders will be confronted with the unprecedented challenge of a regional opponent fully capable of effectively employing WMD, and willing to do so. In fact, this very nearly happened in the Gulf war, although Saddam Hussein ultimately proved unwilling to use the WMD at his disposal.[21] When the United States confronts a challenger with the combination of capability and will, U.S. regional power projection options that previously could be considered low risk, will entail the possibility of military and civilian casualties on a scale far greater than those seen since World War II. The question, then, of how to deter will become paramount. As William Perry, the current secretary of defense, rightly observed in 1991, "Clearly the United States does not want to spend the rest of the decade fighting regional conflicts. The key to avoiding such entanglements is to use its new strength to deter these conflicts rather than fight them."[22]

U.S. government body. The list includes South Africa (which has since eschewed its nuclear weapons program), Argentina, and Brazil, but does not include Libya or Syria.

19. R. James Woolsey in U.S. Senate, Committee on Governmental Affairs, *Proliferation Threats of the 1990's*, 103d Cong., 1st sess. (Washington, D.C.: GPO, 1993), 18.

20. Quoted in Shi Yukun, "Lt. Gen. Li Jijun Answers Questions on Nuclear Deterrence, Nation-state, and Information Age," *China Military Science*, no. 3 (August 1995), 70–76, translated in Foreign Broadcast Information Service, FBIS-CHI-95-236, 8 December 1995, 26.

21. This case is fully examined in Chapter 4.

22. William J. Perry, "Desert Storm and Deterrence," *Foreign Affairs* 70, no. 4 (Fall 1991): 82.

The potential for dramatically higher levels of Western casualties as a result of proliferation is emerging simultaneously with an apparent increase in U.S. sensitivity to losses in power projection operations.[23] It is not difficult to anticipate the impact on U.S. and Western regional defense options if these two trends mature unabated: regional power projection options that were reasonable in the past increasingly will become too risky for the U.S. and its coalition partners—again underscoring the need for effective U.S. policies of deterrence vis-à-vis regional powers.

The picture thus painted of the second nuclear age is not comforting: an international environment characterized by increasing incidence of regional challenges, and greater access by regional powers to WMD. As James Woolsey, former director of the Central Intelligence Agency, observed of the second nuclear age, "we have slain a large dragon. But we live now in a jungle filled with a bewildering variety of poisonous snakes. And in many ways, the dragon was easier to keep track of."[24]

Not surprisingly, for U.S. policy the question of how to deter in this environment has become preeminent. Indeed, as the United States continues to draw down its forces deployed abroad, the requirement for robust regional deterrence policies will increase: the U.S. forces necessary to affect directly events "on the ground" in regional crises will no longer be so readily available.[25]

---

23. This apparent increased U.S. sensitivity to accepting military casualties is discussed in Luttwak, "Toward Post-Heroic Warfare." As General Philippe Morillon, a French commander of the U.N. forces in Bosnia observed, "Desert Storm left one awful legacy. It imposed the idea that you must be able to fight the wars of the future without suffering losses. The idea of zero-kill as an outcome has been imposed on American generals. But there is no such thing as a clean or risk-free war. You condemn yourself to inactivity if you set that standard." Quoted in Jim Hoagland, "Even America Gets the Blues," *Washington Post*, 14 December 1993, A25. In recognition of the requirement to minimize casualties, the Joint Chiefs of Staff have specified that "in all cases, U.S. military forces must be able to undertake operations rapidly, with a high probability of success, and with minimal risk of U.S. casualties." *1993 Joint Military Net Assessment*, unclassified version (Washington, D.C.: Department of Defense, 1993), 3. I thank Kurt Guthe, senior analyst at the National Institute for Public Policy, for bringing to my attention this important point and the statements cited above.

24. Statement before the Senate Select Committee on Intelligence, 2 February 1993, 2 (mimeographed).

25. For example, the number of U.S. overseas air bases has declined dramatically. Since 1960 the number has dropped by 75 percent, from eighty-one major air bases to nineteen in 1995. Most of our remaining bases are in NATO Europe, Japan, and Korea; and popular sentiment in Japan appears to be a growing opposition to hosting U.S. forces and facilities.

In discussions of how to deter in this dramatically new environment, however, many commentators and U.S. officials remain intuitively comfortable with Cold War approaches to deterrence policy. Although expressions of recognition that something has changed are heard, still rare is any serious discussion of how past U.S. nuclear deterrence policies may now be suspect and why, and what may be a better direction for the United States in the second nuclear age. Recent government-sponsored efforts to reexamine U.S. deterrence policy in light of the dramatic changes of the second nuclear age have not escaped the deterrence "old think" of the Cold War. The Pentagon's much-ballyhooed 1994 *Nuclear Posture Review*, as reported, gives little indication of even recognizing that a change might be in order. The much more modest 1991 "Reed Report" did far better in this regard, at least acknowledging that factors important to traditional U.S. deterrence considerations were in flux.[26]

The depth to which now-traditional Cold War deterrence thought has taken root in U.S. policy would be difficult to overstate. Cold War thinking about deterrence was popularized by the 1960s and came to be regarded as a reliable set of general axioms, including the proposition that nuclear deterrence serves to make large-scale war "unthinkable," and largely implausible.[27] More serious and cautionary discussions of the subject, including warnings about the reliability of Cold War deterrence theory as a guide to policy, seemingly have been without effect on U.S. policymakers, in part because those discussions and warnings are bogged down in abstract and technical language. In fact, despite the central role of deterrence in U.S. military strategy, most detailed assessments of deterrence theory have become so abstract

---

26. See U.S. Senate, Committee on Armed Services, *Briefings on Results of the Nuclear Posture Review, Hearings*, 103d Cong., 2d sess. (Washington, D.C.: GPO, 1994); Thomas Reed and Michael Wheeler, *The Role of Nuclear Weapons in the New World Order* (December 1991; mimeographed).

27. Professor Louis Halle presented this widespread view with admirable clarity in 1973; as a result of nuclear deterrence, "Our conclusion, in its narrowest terms, must be that the deliberate resort to war by a nuclear power against a power capable of effective retaliation is permanently ruled out . . . the deliberate resort to major nonnuclear warfare between such powers is also ruled out. And the resort to even such limited warfare as border skirmishes between them is notably inhibited by the danger that it would escalate out of control, ending in nuclear war." See Louis Halle, "Does War Have A Future?" *Foreign Affairs* 52, no. 1 (October 1973): 23.

as to be largely inaccessible to the policy-attentive public, opinion-shaping elites, lawmakers and their staffs, and most incumbents of the White House, State Department, and Department of Defense. Consequently, those simple Cold War axioms about deterrence theory and policy that have achieved widespread recognition now threaten to shape U.S. policy in the second nuclear age, regardless of their applicability (or lack thereof) to the emerging strategic environment.

Before we attempt to establish a framework for considering regional deterrence policies for the future, Cold War deterrence axioms must be reconsidered—in language that does not smother the value of the effort for all but a small handful of specialists in academia. My intention here is to do just that, drawing upon history and historical analysis to help illustrate the fragility of Cold War deterrence thought and to begin the journey toward more useful guidelines for the second nuclear age. I hope that this effort will be of value to the cognoscenti. More so, however, I intend to identify for the attentive public, policy-shapers, and policymakers the mythical qualities of the Cold War thinking about deterrence that has enveloped us and that now threatens to steer our policies in a dangerous direction.

Chapter 2
New Environment, New Requirement

If we had possessed a deterrent—missiles that could reach New York—we would have hit it at the same moment. Consequently, we should build this force so that they and others will no longer think about an attack.

—Mu'ammar Gadhafi, 1990

Implicitly or explicitly, U.S. Cold War deterrence policies focused on U.S.-Soviet relations and presumed a bipolar international en vironment—not unreasonable starting points for the period when the theoretical framework for these policies emerged, the 1950s and 1960s. The Cold War goal of U.S. nuclear deterrence policies was to prevent nuclear and conventional attack against the United States and those allies covered by the U.S. nuclear umbrella. The Soviet Union, with its enormous conventional capabilities poised against Western Europe and its later tremendous nuclear arsenal was the primary source of concern and object of U.S. strategic deterrence threats.

In the second nuclear age, several factors are combining to change the strategic environment and render more challenging the establishment of effective deterrence policies: the apparent in crease in threats posed by rogue states such as Iraq, Iran, Libya, Syria, China, and North Korea;[1] the retraction of U.S. forward-based forces; and the proliferation of WMD. Given these features of the second nuclear age, in comparison to the Cold War, U.S. deterrence goals will have to be expanded: the list of players to be deterred has to be expanded, as do the types of behavior to be prevented.[2]

In this chapter I shall identify the unprecedented character of the threat posed by proliferation in the second nuclear age, and how that threat complicates the deterrence mission.

---

1. So-called rogue states are those that appear willing to flout the "rules of the road" established by the status quo powers and behave in unanticipated ways. They are, therefore, unpredictable and potentially dangerous.

2. The Clinton Administration's Counterproliferation Initiative, for example, includes deterrence as one of the countermeasures necessary to address the threats posed by proliferation. For an introduction to the Department of Defense's Counterproliferation Initiative, see Secretary of Defense Les Aspin, *Annual Report to the President and the Congress* (Washington, D.C.: GPO, January 1994), 34–41.

Proliferation

The trends in missile and WMD proliferation are cause for concern and should be considered together. The threat stems not from the spread of nuclear weapons alone, but also from the spread of chemical and biological weapons and the means to deliver those weapons at long range.

By the end of the 1990s, twenty or more developing countries could acquire missiles overtly or covertly. North Korea has played a central role in missile proliferation. It has sold modified Scud missiles internationally, and seeks international sales of its new 1,000-1,300 km-range Nodong 1 missile, which is capable of carrying conventional and WMD warheads,[3] and reportedly could be deployed in 1996.[4] As the then-director of the CIA remarked of North Korean missile marketing, "It is willing to sell to any country with the cash to pay."[5] North Korea may already have concluded agreements to provide the Nodong 1 to Iran and assistance to Iran in the construction of a Nodong 1 production facility.[6] Libya and Syria also have indicated an interest in the Nodong 1, and Libya is reported to have concluded an agreement to purchase the missile and/or related technologies.[7] If North Korea, Iran, and North African countries ultimately possess the Nodong 1, cities in Japan, France, Italy, Greece, and Turkey could be under the potential threat of missiles armed with WMD.

North Korea has two new multistage missiles in development with considerably greater range than that of the Nodong 1.[8]

---

3. As observed by CIA Director R. James Woolsey in, "US Officials Welcome Delay In N. Korean Missile Sale," *Christian Science Monitor*, 27 December 1993, 4.

4. As cited in Kenneth Katzman and Rinn-Sup Shinn, "North Korea: Military Relations with the Middle East," *CRS Report for Congress*, Congressional Research Service, 27 September 1994, 7.

5. R. James Woolsey in U.S. Senate, Committee on Governmental Affairs, *Proliferation Threats of the 1990's*, 103d Cong., 1st sess. (Washington, D.C.: GPO, 1993), 14.

6. See Joseph Bermudez, "Proliferation for Profit: North Korea in the Middle East," *Policy Focus*, Washington Research Memorandum, no. 27 (July 1994): 20–23; and "North Korea Grasps at the Stage beyond Nodong 1," *Jane's Defence Weekly*, 19 March 1994, 18. For a comprehensive review of recent North Korean missile activities, see Keith B. Payne, "Ballistic Missile Proliferation," *The World in Conflict 1994/95, Jane's Intelligence Review* (January 1995): 20–24.

7. As stated in Statement by Joseph Bermudez, House Committee on Foreign Affairs, Subcommittee on International Security, International Organizations and Human Rights, September 1993, 3, 8 (mimeographed).

8. As then-CIA Director Woolsey has recently stated, "We can confirm that the North Koreans are developing two additional missiles with ranges greater than the 1,000

According to public accounts by U.S. intelligence officials, if launched from North Korea these missiles could threaten "all of Northeast Asia, Southeast Asia, much of the Pacific area, and even most of Russia"; if transferred to North Africa and the Middle East, "all the capitals of Europe could be threatened."[9] North Korea's new missiles, popularly referred to as the Taepodong 1 and Taepodong 2, have been identified in unofficial sources as having ranges of 2,000 km and 3,500 to 10,000 km respectively.[10] U.S. senior defense and intelligence officials have stated publicly that the North Korean Taepodong 2, if deployed, would potentially be able to target "Alaska and parts of Hawaii" (suggesting an intercontinental-range missile) and could be operational before the end of the decade.[11] North Korean Kim Myong Chol, former editor of *The People's Korea* and reportedly closely tied to the government in North Korea, has stated that "In less than 10 years,

---

kilometer missile that it flew last year. These new missiles have yet to be flown, and we will monitor their development, including any attempts to export them in the future to countries such as Iran. Unlike the missiles the North Koreans have already tested, these two—if they are developed and flight tested—could put at risk all of Northeast Asia, Southeast Asia and the Pacific area, and if exported to the Middle East, could threaten Europe as well." As stated in Address by Director of Central Intelligence R. James Woolsey, *Intelligence and Democracy: The CIA and American Foreign Policy,* before the Conference on "The Origins and Development of the CIA in the Administration of Harry S. Truman," 17 March 1994, 9 (mimeographed).

9. R. James Woolsey, presentation at the National Defense University series on "BMD, Counter Proliferation, Arms Control and Deterrence," Washington, D.C., 22 June 1994.

10. According to the Monterey Institute of International Studies Program for Nonproliferation Studies "if the solid fuel used is extremely efficient and the payload is reduced, the Taepo Dong-2's range could be as much as 9600 km." Monterey Institute of International Studies, Program for Nonproliferation Studies, "Missile and Space Launch Capabilities of Selected Countries," *Nonproliferation Review* 1, no. 3 (spring–summer 1994): 86. A South Korean publication identifies a range of 10,000 km for the Taepodong 2. See "North Korea's 'Missile Game,'" *Korea Focus* 3, no. 6 (November–December, 1995): 150. See also Barbara Starr, "N. Korea casts a longer shadow with TD-2," *Jane's Defence Weekly,* 12 March 1994, 1; Martin Sieff, "Japan, S. Korea Join Missile Race with N. Korea," *Washington Times,* 24 March 1994, A-12; and "North Korea Grasps at the Stage beyond Nodong-1," *Jane's Defence Weekly,* 19 March 1994, 18. The higher end of such range estimates for the Taepodong-2 would, of course, make it an ICBM capable of targeting the United States. See also Barbara Starr, "North Korean Missile R&D Gains New Pace," *Jane's Defence Weekly,* 25 June 1994, 10; and "North Korea's 'Missile Game,'" 150.

11. See the statement by Dr. John Deutch, then-deputy secretary of defense, in U.S. Senate, Committee on Armed Services, *Military Implications of the Chemical Weapons Convention: Hearings,* 103d Cong., 2d sess. (Washington, D.C.: GPO, 1994), 81; and see the answer for the record by Admiral William Studeman, Acting Director of Central Intelligence, U.S. Senate, Select Committee on Intelligence, *Worldwide Intelligence Review: Hearings,* 104th Cong., 1st sess. (Washington, D.C.: GPO, 1995), 105.

North Korea will likely deploy an operational intercontinental ballistic missile force capable of hitting the American mainland."[12]

According to public statements by then-director of the CIA James Woolsey, the direct WMD/missile threat to the United States from proliferant states could develop "after the turn of the century." Woolsey added that there exist certain "shortcuts" to ICBM (intercontinental ballistic missile) acquisition that, "would, of course, speed up ICBM acquisition by such nations."[13]

The emerging threat posed by the proliferation of missiles and WMD has recently received international attention. Both NATO and the Western European Union (WEU) have expressed mounting concern about the danger posed by proliferation. NATO's 1991 Rome Summit, for example, included an agreed statement by the heads of state that the risk posed by "the proliferation of ballistic missiles and weapons of mass destruction should be given special consideration." And the January 1994 NATO Summit in Brussels included direction by the heads of states to "intensify and expand NATO's political and defense efforts against proliferation" and for the development of an overall NATO policy framework to meet the proliferation threat.

The proliferation threat confronting Japan and the southern portions of Europe is more immediate than that to U.S. territory. The much-noted North Korean missile and WMD programs could, for example, place Japan at additional risk in the very near future. Former Japanese Prime Minister Kiichi Miyazawa labeled this possibility a "grave concern."[14] It has led to some comments

---

12. "North Korea Prepared to Fight to the End as Kim Jong-il Has His Own Version of *The Art of War*," *Asia Times*, 10 April 1996, 9.

13. See Woolsey, *Proliferation Threats of the 1990s*, 28. More recently, with regard to the possible time frame for additional long-range missile threats to the United States, Woolsey observed that the United States could "assemble a small technical 'red team' of bright young American scientists and engineers and let them see what could be assembled from internationally available technology and components. I would bet that we would be shocked at what they could show us about available capabilities in ballistic missiles." See *Statement of R. James Woolsey, before the House Committee on National Security*, 14 March 1996, 5 (mimeographed).

14. "Miyazawa Calls DPRK Nuclear Development "Direct Threat,'" *Yomiuri Shimbun*, 7 June 1993, 2. And a 12 August 1994 report by the Prime Minister's Advisory Group on Defense Issues identifies the potential for "limited missile attack" as a threat of particular importance. See Advisory Group on Defense Issues, *The Modality of the Security and Defense Capability of Japan: The Outlook for the 21st Century*, 12 August 1994, 18. For a more detailed review of the Japanese response to North Korean developments, see Payne, "Ballistic Missile Proliferation" and idem, "Proliferation and Counterproliferation: An American View," *Kaigai Jijyo Journal of World Affairs* (Takushoku University, Tokyo) 42, no. 7–8 (July–August 1994): 54–73.

by senior Japanese officials about the once-unmentionable: Japanese development of nuclear capabilities. On 28 July 1993, for example, Japanese Foreign Minister Kabun Muto observed that North Korean programs could compel the Japanese to build nuclear weapons if necessary: "If North Korea develops nuclear weapons and that becomes a threat to Japan, first, there is the nuclear umbrella of the United States upon which we can rely. But if it comes down to a crunch, possessing the will that 'we can do it' is important."[15]

This statement seems to be consistent with recent press accounts of a 1969 top-secret Japanese report entitled *Prerequisites of Japan's Foreign Policy.* This document reportedly states that Japan would "maintain the economic and technical potential of producing nuclear weapons," but "for the time being, we will adopt a policy of not possessing nuclear arms."[16] Such an approach seems to leave room for Japanese nuclear arms if conditions necessitate a serious reorientation of security policies. It should be noted, however, that there also have been clear Japanese statements concerning Japan's intention to remain non-nuclear.[17]

Two points are suggested by this discussion. First, of course, is that proliferation is beginning to pose a real threat to U.S. allies and overseas interests. Second, proliferation can be self-propelled, as proliferation by one regional power serves as the catalyst for further proliferation in that region—the pressure on Japan from North Korean proliferation demonstrating the point. Consequently, the view noted above by Kabun Muto concerning

---

15. Quoted in "Japan Spells Out Nuclear Stance," *Los Angeles Times*, 29 July 1993, p. A-18. See also Martin Sieff, "Japan Mulls Atomic Weapons to Deter Nuclear Neighbors," *Washington Times*, 10 November 1993, A-13.

Japanese concern about North Korean intentions is understandable. The North Korean ambassador in New Delhi reportedly stated that "our nuclear arms, if developed, would be primarily designed to contain Japan." Quoted in "DPRK Ambassador to India Interviewed," FBIS-EAS-94-066, 6 April 1994, 32. And, in a separate but similar development, former North Korean Army 1st Lieutenant Yim Yong-son, who defected to South Korea in September 1993, stated that North Korea had begun to build missile launch sites near the border with China in the belief that the United States would not strike at sites near the Chinese border. See "North Missile Sites Said Along PRC Border" in FBIS-EAS-94-068, 8 April 1994, 32.

16. The Japanese Foreign Ministry acknowledged the report. As reported in, Eugene Moosa, "Japanese Started Nuclear Plan in '69," *Washington Times*, 5 August 1994, A14.

17. The August 1994 report by the prime minister's Advisory Group on Defense Issues states that Japan "is determined to firmly maintain its nonnuclear policy." See Advisory Group on Defense Issues, *The Modality of the Security and Defense Capability of Japan: The Outlook for the 21st Century*, 16.

Japanese armament, despite the furor it stirred, should not come as a surprise. Japan is a country with a high population density, and a small number of North Korean missiles and WMD could place much of the Japanese population and industry at risk.

Direct Threats of Proliferation

Recognition of the emerging threat posed by proliferation worldwide is one reason why the Clinton administration elevated counterproliferation as a priority American goal. The second nuclear age will be characterized by the direct threats posed by proliferation and the potential for intimidation from sources new to the second nuclear age and possibly severe, depending on the specific circumstances. These direct threats, and those intended to intimidate, will have the potential to paralyze U.S. regional defense options by putting U.S. power projection forces at risk, and ultimately by putting U.S. urban centers at risk. Past cases, including the Gulf war, the Cuban missile crisis, and German missile attacks against Britain in World War II illustrate these different threats.

The near-term direct threat to Western military forces and urban centers is the most obvious. Unless countered, the proliferation of WMD and delivery means, including ballistic missiles and cruise missiles, will introduce a situation unknown to the Cold War: Western expeditionary forces will confront regional opponents capable of striking rapidly at cities, seaports, airports, and troop concentrations with nuclear, chemical, and biological weapons. This emerging capability may render the United States increasingly vulnerable to deterrence and coercive threats by otherwise second- and third-rate regional powers, given the emerging heightened U.S. sensitivity to casualties. WMD and missile proliferation could thus undermine the West's capacity to mount force projection operations at an acceptable level of risk and the West's capacity to respond to regional aggression when necessary.

The direct military significance of such a development for the international order is perhaps best understood by considering whether Desert Shield or Desert Storm would have been feasible had Saddam Hussein used missiles and WMD to strike the sea and airports used by Coalition forces. Clearly, the six-month buildup of Coalition forces to protect Saudi Arabia and subsequently to liberate Kuwait would have been extraordinarily risky,

perhaps impossible, in the face of WMD strikes on regional airports, seaports, and troop concentrations. In short, U.S. force
projection could become exceedingly risky as ports, airports, troop
and matériel concentrations become increasingly vulnerable to
WMD.

World War II provides an early example of how missiles in the
hands of an aggressor could have had disastrous consequences for
expeditionary forces. The German development of missiles during
World War II posed a potential threat to allied expeditionary
forces: commenting on the German V-1 and V-2 missiles, Supreme
Allied Commander Gen. Dwight D. Eisenhower noted soon after
the war that "it seemed likely that, if the German had succeeded
in perfecting and using these new weapons six months earlier
than he did, our invasion of Europe would have proved exceedingly difficult, perhaps impossible. I feel sure that if he had
succeeded in using these weapons over a six-month period, and
particularly if he had made the Portsmith-Southampton area one
of his principal targets, Overlord might have been written off."[18]
This type of missile threat will exist within the foreseeable future
in virtually any region where Western expeditionary forces might
realistically be needed, and that threat will be magnified by the
likely presence of WMD.

The Gulf war also demonstrated the terror value of direct
threats by "militarily insignificant" missiles (missiles without
sufficient accuracy or lethality to threaten military targets). Scud
missiles, for example, while of little direct military use during the
Gulf war, ultimately served Saddam Hussein as weapons of terror. In this capacity they diverted a fairly significant air effort to
the "Scud hunt," despite the fact that according to the Air Force's
Gulf War Air Power Survey, most, maybe even all, of the mobile
Scud launchers reported destroyed were either decoys or other
objects.[19] They also threatened to tear the Coalition apart
politically by bringing Israel into the war and thereby splitting
Arab states away from the U.S.-led Coalition.

World War II again provides an example of this potential military significance of militarily insignificant weapons. The British
air campaign to counter Germany's similarly "militarily insignifi-

---

18.   Dwight D. Eisenhower, *Crusade in Europe* (New York: Doubleday, 1948), 260.

19.   *Gulf War Air Power Survey*, vol. 11, *Operations* (Washington, D.C.: GPO, 1993),
179–91.

cant" V-1 and V-2 missiles diverted considerable British military capability and ultimately led to the loss of 450 British aircraft and approximately 2,900 air personnel.[20] The lesson had to be learned anew during the Gulf war: politically significant terror threats to the population, even if militarily insignificant, can easily compel a diversion of military assets that in itself could become militarily significant.

In the future, unless countered, missiles are likely to have both a similar second-order military impact and—when mated with WMD—the potential for a much more significant direct military effect, rendering future operations such as Desert Shield or Desert Storm much more dangerous or impossible. The direct threat, however, will not be limited to possible strikes against Western expeditionary forces. Countries geographically close to regional bullies armed with WMD, for example, may face the possibility of WMD strikes against their urban centers in the foreseeable future. Some U.S. allies and friends face this prospect now, or soon will, including South Korea, Japan, and Israel.

The impact of such a direct threat on civilians and political leaders, even if the threat involves "only" chemical weapons and crude missiles, can be understood in part by reference to the tremendous strain Israel confronted when its urban centers were under attack by Scud missiles and the *possibility* of chemical warheads. Actual chemical strikes against unprotected civilian centers could involve enormous casualty levels.[21] The British World War II experience with the V-1 and V-2 missiles is instructive. Strikes by these missiles, armed only with conventional warheads, inflicted 67,111 casualties, damaged or destroyed two million houses, and—with the V-2 in particular—had a very damaging effect on British public morale.[22]

20. For a detailed examination of the British World War II experience with German V-1 and V-2 attacks, see Robin Ranger, "Theater Missile Defenses: Lessons from British Experiences with Air and Missile Defenses," *Comparative Strategy* 12, no. 4 (October–December 1993): 405–7.

21. And, as Woolsey has noted with regard to biological weapons, "Bacteriological warheads in particular will serve about as well as nuclear ones for purposes of turning a country's ballistic missiles into extremely effective tools of terror and blackmail, even if they are never launched." See *Statement of R. James Woolsey, before the House Committee on National Security*, 3.

22. Ranger, "Theater Missile Defense," 405–7.

Intimidation

The potential for intimidation made possible by proliferation involves the effect the threat of missile and WMD strikes would likely have on Western leaders' willingness to accept the risk of projecting forces in response to regional crises and aggression. In the future, regional military operations that hitherto have been considered reasonable options, such as the war to liberate Kuwait, British recovery of the Falkland Islands, or French support for Chad against Libya, could become too risky to be considered politically acceptable. The option to engage in such force projection operations, if involving the possibility of opponents' WMD, could be dismissed out of hand. Even the humanitarian use of military force, such as that conducted under the auspices of the UN in Somalia, or the rescue of nationals or foreign citizens from a dangerous overseas situation, could be considered too risky. Again, the significance of a proliferant state's potential to constrain Western decision-making so dramatically may be understood by consideration of the Coalition war with Iraq. If Iraq had been capable of threatening Washington, London, Paris, and Rome with WMD, it might have been able to deter any forceful Western response whatsoever to the invasion of Kuwait.

The West has in the past been willing and capable of projecting force when necessary in response to regional aggression. In the future, proliferation could provide regional bullies and aggressors with a free hand. Such a development would have a disastrous effect on U.S. allies and friends who confront proliferant neighbors. Concern that proliferation could undermine the West's capability and will to respond to regional crises and leave it vulnerable to deterrence and coercion is not speculative. The 1962 Cuban missile crisis demonstrates how U.S. military options were dramatically constrained by the presence of WMD and missiles—in an area, it should be noted, of overwhelming U.S. conventional force superiority.

During the Cuban missile crisis the chance that U.S. air strikes against the missile sites in Cuba would not destroy all of the missiles—and that surviving missiles and nuclear weapons could be launched at the United States—significantly limited the military options Kennedy considered "acceptable." Kennedy believed that "if we come and attack, they're going to fire them."[23] In short, *in part* because Lieutenant General Sweeney, at the time commander of the U.S. Tactical Air Command, acknowledged that an air strike could not be guaranteed to "get 'em all,"[24] the option of destroying the missile sites in Cuba was considered unacceptable by the political leadership.[25]

The probability of nuclear escalation was thought at the time to be relatively low—one in fifty, according to Secretary of Defense McNamara. Nevertheless, although the probability seemed low, the U.S. political leadership understandably was unwilling to accept that level of risk when "millions of American deaths" could have resulted.[26] As McNamara stated in this regard, "I wasn't willing to accept that risk. And I know the President wasn't willing to accept it. And I'm talking about one nuclear bomb on one American city. That's all."[27]

Unknown to U. S. leaders at the time, but clear now, is that immediately prior to the outbreak of the crisis, Soviet forces on Cuba had been delegated authority to use nuclear weapons against U.S. forces in response to an American invasion of the island. While that authority later was withdrawn, senior Soviet military officers believe that there continued to be a serious prospect for Soviet nuclear use in the event of U.S. invasion of the island.[28] Indeed, at least some on the Soviet side anticipated that in the event of an invasion, "the Americans would have lost more

---

23.   James Blight and David Welch, *On the Brink: Americans and Soviets Reexamine the Cuban Missile Crisis* (New York: Hill and Wang, 1989), 349. In the same source, Dean Rusk states, "Well, the trouble with an air strike, if the missile sites were operational, was that there was no guarantee that you'd get them all. There's a possibility you'll have some strikes against the United States. You see, the Air Force was asked about this and they could not guarantee that they would get all the sites. They might get 85 to 90 percent of them, but they wouldn't get them all. And this was an important point to President Kennedy" (176).

24.   Ibid., 80. See also *Document 25: Secretary of Defense Robert McNamara, Military Briefing, Notes on October 21, 1962 Meeting with the President,* in, *The Cuban Missile Crisis, 1962: A National Security Archive Documents Reader,* ed. Laurence Chang and Peter Kornbluh (New York: New York Univ. Press, 1962), 145; and Raymond Garthoff, *Reflections on the Cuban Missile Crisis* (Washington, D.C.: Brookings Institution, 1989), 49–50.

25.   Donald Kagan, although concluding that additional factors were at work, presents some evidence supporting this point in his case study of the Cuban missile crisis. See Donald Kagan, *On the Origins of War* (New York: Doubleday, 1995), 510–18.

26.   Blight and Welch, *On the Brink*, 88.

27.   Ibid., 193; see also 57.

28.   See General Anatoli Gribkov, "The View from Moscow and Havana," in, General Anatoli Gribkov and General William Smith, *Operation ANADYR: U.S. and Soviet Generals Recount the Cuban Missile Crisis* (Chicago: edition q, 1994), 5.

than they lost during the whole [of] World War II," and Soviet forces would have been annihilated in the U.S. response.[29]

The Cuban missile crisis is a real-world example of the powerfully constraining effect that even a limited WMD and missile threat can have on the willingness and capacity of American leaders to act forcefully in support of Western interests. It may serve as a valuable case study when considering future U.S. counterproliferation options.

The value of ballistic missiles and WMD for deterrence and coercion of American leaders is anticipated by the political and military leaders of some proliferant states. As a South Korean assessment of the North Korean Nodong and Taepodong 2 missiles concludes, "North Korea seems to be using its missile capability as diplomatic leverage by aiming its 1,000 km–2,000 km missiles at Japan, and [will aim] its 10,000 km missiles at the United States. . . . North Korea, which has already benefited by playing its 'nuclear card,' may reap a bumper harvest in its missile game, as well."[30] In discussing North Korea's concept of how to deter U.S. leaders, Kim Myong Chol makes the striking observation that "Supreme Commander Kim Jong-il" can demonstrate that war with North Korea would be "futile" by, among other steps, having "brutal war scenes broadcast live to the U.S. mainland" and by launching "long-range ballistic missiles with super-bomb warheads at a few prime strategic targets in Japan and the United States, such as nuclear power stations and major metropolitan centers like New York and Washington."[31]

Remarks by both Saddam Hussein and Colonel Gadhafi also are instructive in this regard. Months before the invasion of Kuwait, Saddam Hussein expressed a deterrent theme with regard to Israel by stating that if Israel ever "tries to do anything against Iraq," Iraqi chemical weapons would "make the fire eat up half of Israel."[32] Gadhafi sounded a similar deterrent/coercive theme in response to the 1986 U.S. air strikes against Tripoli and Benghazi: "Did not the Americans almost hit you . . . when you were asleep

---

29. See the discussion by Sergo Mikoyan and crisis participants in "The Missiles of October: What the World Didn't Know," ABC News, 17 October 1992, Transcript ABC-40, 24.

30. "North Korea's 'Missile Game,'" 150.

31. Chol, "North Korea Prepared to Fight," 9.

32. Quoted in Alan Cowell, "Iraq Chief, Boasting of Poison Gas, Warns of Disaster if Israelis Strike," *New York Times*, 3 April 1990, A1.

in your homes? If they know that you have a deterrent force capable of hitting the United States, they would not be able to hit you. If we had possessed a deterrent—missiles that could reach New York—we would have hit it at the same moment. Consequently, we should build this force so that they and others will no longer think about an attack."[33]

Former Indian Army Chief of Staff General K. Sundarji reportedly endorsed missiles and WMD for the purpose of establishing a "minimum deterrent" to discourage "U.S. bullying" and "possible racist aggression from the West."[34] Sundarji reportedly expressed a prevalent Indian view when he observed that India requires a nuclear deterrent "to dissuade big powers from lightly pursuing policies of compellance vis-à-vis India. The Gulf War emphasized once again that nuclear weapons are the ultimate coin of power. In the final analysis, they [Coalition members] could go in because the United States had nuclear weapons and Iraq didn't."[35]

Missiles and WMD are also viewed as possible tools of coercion against the United States. As Abu Abbas, head of the Palestine Liberation Front and terrorist mastermind of the 1985 hijacking of the *Achille Lauro*, noted in reaction to U.S. initiatives during the crisis preceding the Gulf war, "revenge takes forty years; if not my son, then the son of my son will kill you. Some day, we will have missiles that can reach New York."[36] And "I would love to be able to reach the American shore, but this is very difficult. . . . Some day an Arab country will have ballistic missiles. Some day an Arab country will have a nuclear bomb. It is better for the United States and for Israel to reach peace with the Palestinians before that day."[37]

33. Speech by Gadhafi at a meeting of students of the Higher Institute for Applied Social Studies at the Great al-Fatih University, 18 April 1990, Tripoli Television Service, 19 April 1990 (trans. in Foreign Broadcast Information Service, *Daily Report: Near East & South Asia*, FBIS-NES-90-078, 23 April 1990, 8).

34. Translated in Foreign Broadcast Information Service, *Daily Report: Near East and South Asia* (FBIS-NES-92-199), 14 October 1992, 46.

35. Quoted in Selig Harrison and Geoffrey Kemp, *India and America after the Cold War* (Washington, D.C.: Carnegie Endowment for International Peace, 1993), 20.

36. Quoted in Tony Horwitz, "A Terrorist Talks about Life, Warns of More Deaths," *Wall Street Journal*, 10 September 1990, p. 1.

37. Quoted in Marie Colvin, "Terror Chief Threatens Onslaught in Europe," *London Sunday Times*, 23 September 1990, 2.

In early 1996 Chinese officials engaged in missile threats for deterrence and coercive purposes, and ultimately launched unarmed missiles into international waters very near Taiwan in an admitted effort to intimidate Taiwanese voters as they prepared for Taiwan's first-ever democratic presidential elections. In addition, according to reports by former Assistant Secretary of Defense Charles Freeman, the Chinese People's Liberation Army completed plans to launch a missile per day against Taiwan for one month to coerce Taiwan away from its recent drive for "independent international status." Chinese officials are reported by Freeman as claiming that the United States would not intervene in such a crisis because American leaders "care more about Los Angeles than they do about Taiwan"—clearly indicating a belief that the United States could be deterred from involvement by the Chinese nuclear missile threat to Los Angeles.[38] Winston Lord, a senior U.S. State Department official, similarly reported that Chinese officials claimed that the United States would not "dare to defend Taiwan" from Chinese attack because China would "rain nuclear bombs on Los Angeles." Lord labeled these Chinese threats "psychological warfare."[39] They caused the stock market in Taipei to plummet temporarily, and the missile tests near Taiwan's shores amounted to a several-day partial blockade of Taiwan's major ports.[40]

Obviously, the potential value of missile threats for deterrence, coercion, and intimidation of U.S. leaders is valued by terrorist and rogue leaders. Again, the Cuban missile crisis may be instructive. In his exhaustive recent study of this crisis, Donald Kagan concludes that the primary reason Premier Khrushchev risked placing missiles and nuclear weapons in Cuba was because he believed they would reduce the U.S. will to confront the Soviet Union. Soviet missiles in Cuba would help free the Soviet Union from the discipline of U.S. nuclear threats in regional contingencies and thereby provide the basis for more activist

---

38. This disturbing development is reported in Patrick Tyler, "As China Threatens Taiwan, It Makes Sure U.S. Listens," *New York Times*, 24 January 1996, A3. See also "China Threatens Taiwan," *New York Times*, 25 January 1995, A20; and Charles Freeman, "The End of Taiwan?" *New York Times*, 15 February 1996, A27.

39. Report by Jim Wolf, Reuter 23:36 EST, 17 March 1996, 1.

40. "China Keeps Tensions High on Taiwan," *Washington Times*, 26 January 1996, A14. See also the discussion in Woolsey, *Statement of R. James Woolsey, before the House Committee on National Security*, 1.

Soviet regional initiatives.[41] With even a modest nuclear threat against the United States in place, according to Kagan, Khrushchev anticipated being more confident that U.S. leaders would be unwilling to respond forcefully to Soviet regional provocations because of the attendant nuclear risk. "Khrushchev did not want to launch a first strike or any nuclear strike at all. What he wanted was a credible nuclear force that would paralyze the Americans. . . . It was based on Khrushchev's conviction that the Americans would not use nuclear weapons if, as McNamara later enthusiastically affirmed, there was any chance of *some* nuclear weapons falling on the United States."[42]

This lesson of the Cuban missile crisis should not be lost. Clearly the deterrent and even coercive value of ballistic missiles and WMD, particularly against the United States, is attractive to some of those currently seeking to create or acquire them. Some developing countries seek WMD and missiles to enable them to hold the advanced Western powers at bay through deterrence while pursuing whatever regional policies they might choose. This potential capability to deter and coerce is likely to be motive enough for some aspiring proliferant countries to pursue WMD and missiles.

It should be noted that establishing such a deterrent/coercive capability against the United States would *not* require that a challenger actually be willing to initiate a WMD attack against the United States. Rather, the mere possession of missiles and WMD by regional aggressors would compel Western leaders to consider the risks—with the consequent inhibitions on the options Western leaders could consider acceptable.

It is this potential U.S. vulnerability to regional powers' policies of deterrence and coercion, backed by WMD, that is a potentially defining feature of the second nuclear age. In many ways, whether the leader of a rogue regional power actually would dare a WMD strike against the United States is an important albeit secondary issue; more important is the potentially paralyzing effect on U.S. leaders the possibility of such a strike could have, and the potential for the threat to constitute a tool for regional

---

41. Kagan, *On the Origins of War*, 511, 513. That this goal of being freed from the U.S. nuclear deterrent restrictions in regional initiatives was a key element of "peaceful coexistence" is presented in Keith B. Payne, "Are They Interested in Stability? The Soviet View of Peaceful Coexistence," *Comparative Strategy* 3, no. 1 (1981): 1–24.

42. Donald Kagan, *On the Origins of War*, 511–12.

challengers to coerce and deter the United States and its allies—
dramatically limiting U.S. options in regional crises.

U.S. Deterrence Policies: New Requirements

Many prominent commentators claim that rogue challengers
would, in fact, "never dare" to use WMD against U.S. targets because of the certainty of a devastating U.S. nuclear response.[43]
That is, U.S. nuclear deterrence is expected to prevent rogue use of
missiles and WMD against U.S. territory.[44] This expectation may
be warranted in many cases. In other cases, however, to be so
effective U.S. policies of deterrence may have to carry a much
heavier burden than they did during the Cold War. That the
deterrence mission could on occasion be more stressful in the second nuclear age may seem curious given the enormous Cold War
nuclear arsenal of the Soviet Union as compared to the much-
smaller expected missile and WMD arsenals of the rogues. But the
size of the opponent's WMD arsenal is not the issue here; it is the
context in which U.S. policies of deterrence would be expected to
work. In the second nuclear age, that context may, in some
instances, render effective deterrence much more challenging than
was the case during the Cold War.

Cold War nuclear deterrence policies were expected to prevent
Soviet conventional and nuclear aggression against the United
States and its key allies. Deterrence in the second nuclear age will,
on occasion, involve the goal of preventing WMD strikes against
the United States and its allies, even as a U.S.-led coalition is engaged in hostilities on the challenger's territory. Deterrence, in this
case, will not merely have to prevent an opponent from initiating

---

43. It should be recalled, however, that according to former Bush administration
officials, including the president, the United States would *not* have responded with nuclear
weapons had Iraq used chemical and biological weapons in the Gulf war. See President
Bush's statements in *A Gulf War Exclusive: President Bush Talking with David Frost*, Transcript
no. 51, 16 January 1996, 5. Robert Gates, then Director of Central Intelligence has stated that
in response to Iraqi WMD use the United States "would simply expand [the Iraqi] target
base significantly and damage Iraq and the civilian infrastructure and the economy much
worse than we were under that war plan." General Colin Powell has stated that the U.S.
response to Iraqi WMD use could have involved the conventional targeting of the dams on
the Tigris and Euphrates Rivers, flooding Baghdad. See, respectively, the statements by
Robert Gates, in *Frontline*, "The Gulf War, Parts I and II," 9 and 10 January 1996,
background materials available via Internet Web Site www.wgbh.org; and statement of
General Colin Powell, in *Frontline*, "The Gulf War, Part II," no. 1408, 10 January 1996,
transcript, 5.

44. See the detailed discussion of this assertion in Chapter 3.

or escalating conflict against the United States and its allies during a crisis, as was expected of Cold War deterrence policies. It also will have to deter a challenger's strikes while U.S. and allied forces are conducting successful military operations on the challenger's home soil. The opposing leadership in such a case could be desperate, witnessing the destruction of its military and fearing for its own survival. In these circumstances the stakes involved for the challenger's leadership could not be higher.

This deterrence mission is not simply a replay of the Cold War need for "intra-war deterrence." Because actually waging full-scale war against the Soviet Union would have been so dangerous, if deterrence initially failed, U.S. plans included attempts to continue manipulating limited nuclear threats during the war so as to reestablish deterrence—intra-war deterrence. In contrast, in future regional conflicts, U.S. forces could be on a foe's territory, physically destroying the opponent's military and challenging a desperate opposing leadership's very survival, while the United States would simultaneously be attempting to deter that leadership's WMD use. The distinction here between deterring Soviet initiation or escalation of attack and deterring a rogue challenger's use of its WMD is significant. In the first case, U.S. and NATO deterrence policies were expected to cause Soviet leaders to choose to stand down rather than initiate or—if deterrence failed initially—escalate a conflict. Yet, these policies were expected to work in the absence of U.S. forces simultaneously being on Warsaw Pact or Soviet territory destroying the Soviet military establishment and challenging the leadership's political survival. Indeed, U.S. intra-war deterrence threats were intended specifically to communicate limitation to prevent Soviet acts of desperation, and, for the same reason, NATO policies specifically rejected the notion of taking Warsaw Pact territory, eschewing even the appearance that NATO prepared for cross-border operations to do so. Expecting a regional power not to use its deterrent capabilities in response to an impending defeat at the hands of U.S. expeditionary forces would be akin to having expected Soviet leaders not to use their strategic weapons as NATO forces closed in on Moscow. Soviet leaders might have chosen not to do so, but the deterrence of leaders in such desperate circumstances can hardly be assumed.

U.S. deterrence policies of the second nuclear age will, of course, be called on to prevent rogue challengers from initiating or escalating an attack against the United States. Those policies, however, on occasion may have to accomplish this in the very stressing context described above; the challenger essentially would have to be willing to suffer military defeat by U.S. expeditionary forces and the manifest possibility of its own political demise, while remaining deterred from using its WMD.

To expect that a desperate challenger would not resort to its most potent weapons in this context is a tall order. In fact, NATO's Cold War doctrine of "Flexible Response" was predicated on the assumption that deterrence, including nuclear deterrence, could not be expected to operate reliably in such circumstances. Here I am referring to the limitations assumed by NATO to affect the *Soviet* capability to deter NATO nuclear escalation following Soviet attack, assumed limitations that were at the very heart of the Flexible Response doctrine. Indeed, Flexible Response was built on the widely accepted proposition that Soviet leaders could *not* count of deterring NATO nuclear escalation during the heat of a desperate war on NATO territory. Soviet anticipation of NATO nuclear escalation, NATO's "first use," was expected to deter Soviet conventional attack against Western territory—even though WMD escalation by NATO might have served little purpose and would have led to a devastating Soviet WMD reply.[45]

In contrast, in the second nuclear age a comparable U.S. regional nuclear deterrence policy would have to be based on faith in the very different proposition that the opponent would consciously deny itself the use of its foremost weapons while possibly suffering defeat at home. In such a case we will have to ask more of our deterrence capabilities than we assumed the Soviet Union could ask of its deterrence capabilities during the Cold War and in the context of the Warsaw Pact's conventional superiority in Central Europe. If we expected Soviet leaders to discount their capability to deter NATO nuclear escalation while fighting on NATO territory, can we now expect our own deterrence policies of the second nuclear age to give us such a capability vis-à-vis

---

45. It should be noted that evidence now available out of the former East Germany indicates that had war in Europe occurred, the Soviet Union would have *begun* with very heavy use of nuclear and chemical weapons. See Lothar Rühl, "Noch 1990 Zielte die NVA Richtung Westdeutschland und Benelux," *Die Welt*, 31 July 1991, 1; Lothar Rühl, "Angriffskrieger Markus Wolf," *Die Welt*, 9 August 1991; Lothar Rühl, "Offensive Defence in the Warsaw Pact," *Survival* 33, no. 5 (September–October 1991): 442–50. See also Beatrice Heuser, "Warsaw Pact Military Doctrines in the 1970s and 1980s: Findings in the East German Archives," *Comparative Strategy* 12, no. 4 (winter 1994): 437–58.

regional rogues? Should we not anticipate that developing countries will follow NATO's own Cold War model: unwilling or unable to compete at the conventional force level, we ultimately
counted on the deterring effect of nuclear weapons as the means
of holding Soviet conventional power at bay. Recent North Korean
efforts to acquire WMD and missiles capable of targeting U.S. installations in the Pacific, and eventually the United States itself,
certainly appear to reflect a similar North Korean strategy to
counter the superior conventional arms of the West.

In short, Flexible Response was built on the proposition that
Soviet leaders ultimately would not take conventional war to the
West because of the possibility of Western escalation to WMD use.
In contrast, our deterrence policies toward rogue challengers in
the second nuclear age will need somehow to free U.S. leaders
from a challenger's threat of WMD escalation. Our policies will
have to enable U.S. leaders to do what we assumed Soviet Cold
War leaders would not: project overwhelming force into the
opponent's territory without being deterred by the possibility of
the opponent's escalation to WMD. U.S. force projection
requirements in the second nuclear age will include this
unprecedented need for the capability to "deter their deterrent."[46]
In principle at least, this is a more stressing mission than was
expected of our Cold War deterrence and intra-war deterrence
policies.

In sum, when considering U.S. deterrence policies for the second nuclear age, we must recognize that some of the prominent
features of this new age may affect the duties required of those
policies and the capability and will of U.S. leaders to project force
to regional theaters. Most prominent, U.S. deterrence goals would
appear at least to be complicated by the number of potential
regional challengers and their access to WMD and delivery means.

It seems unlikely that U.S. leaders could confidently rely on
policies of deterrence to convince a regional challenger to accept
the possibility of military defeat on its home soil and its own
demise without resorting to its WMD.[47] If U.S. leaders cannot be so

---

46.   In the mid-1970s Paul Nitze warned that the Soviet Union was in the process of
acquiring such a capability vis-à-vis the United States. See "Deterring Our Deterrent,"
Foreign Policy, no. 25 (Winter 1976–77): 195–210.

47.   One of the conclusions reached by Richard Ned Lebow and Janice Gross Stein in
their review of superpower relations in the Yom Kippur and Cuban missile crises suggests
that we may be disappointed if we expect that the U.S. threat of retaliation will predictably
deter a regional rogue's escalation to WMD in the midst of a conventional conflict: "When

confident in their deterrence policies, or cannot counter a rogue's WMD reliably through other mechanisms, they will, at least on those occasions, face a powerful inhibition on projecting U.S. forces.

Whether the United States will see a need to project its forces frequently or rarely in the second nuclear age is an important but separate issue. My interest here is in pointing out that proliferation may enable rogue challengers to deter U.S. force projection options that have, in the past, been taken for granted. And that effectively countering a rogue's threat of WMD escalation, "deterring their deterrent," may on occasion constitute a much more stressful mission than we confronted during the Cold War. James Woolsey's colorful description of the post–Cold War world as "a jungle filled with a bewildering variety of poisonous snakes" is apt. The questions that arise are whether and how we can deter in this "jungle," and whether our Cold War deterrence policies provide useful guidance.

---

unfavorable and they had no grounds to doubt their adversary's resolve." *We All Lost the Cold War* (Princeton: Princeton Univ. Press, 1995), 361.

Chapter 3
The Valor of Ignorance

I am assuming that deterrence will work with these countries as it worked with Josef Stalin and Chairman Mao: 'We'll turn you into a sea of radioactive glass 20 minutes later.'

—John Pike, Federation of American Scientists, 1995

In Chapter 2, I concluded that U.S. effort at deterrence in the second nuclear age may, in some cases, be more complex because of the need to expand the potential list of target states, and because of the expanded duties of deterrence likely to be required. Yet, despite the dramatic changes in the international environment occurring since the late 1980s, many civilian and military specialists who focus on deterrence policy are reluctant to reconsider Cold War deterrence concepts and policies. As Fred Iklé has recently observed in this regard, "The demise of the Soviet empire ought to have made it easier to develop strategies that would complement or, where necessary, substitute for deterrence. Yet the weapons arsenals and intellectual mindset that constitute the Cold War's enormous detritus have obstructed the search for new policies."[1]

This reluctance to consider deterrence anew appears to reflect a general comfort with those existing concepts and policies considered by many to be a proven success. After all, did not U.S. deterrence policies work vis-à-vis the Soviet Union throughout the Cold War? We know that the U.S. intention was to deter conflict; we know that there was no direct conflict with the Soviet Union. It is easy, therefore, to conclude, that U.S. nuclear deterrence policies must have worked and that our understanding of how to deter must be substantial. The problem in linking claims of past deterrence success to expectations for the future, however, in addition to the new opponents and changed circumstances of the

---

1. Fred Charles Iklé, "The Second Coming of the Nuclear Age," *Foreign Affairs* 75, no. 1 (January–February 1996): 119.

second nuclear age, is that reasons other than nuclear deterrence may explain the absence of a Soviet attack during the Cold War. The absence of an attack does not prove that Soviet leaders would have pursued a provocation but were deterred from doing so after weighing the U.S. nuclear retaliatory threat. Their apparent restraint may have reflected any number of possible causes: a lack of confidence in Soviet forces, a general cautiousness with regard to war following the destruction of World War II, or simply little desire to challenge the U.S. directly.[2]

Demonstrating that U.S. policies of nuclear deterrence were effective in preventing Soviet attack throughout the Cold War is impossible in the absence of credible evidence about Soviet intentions and decisions during the period.[3] Intuitively, it seems very likely that U.S. nuclear deterrence policies did contribute abundantly to the prevention of Soviet aggression both in general and on specific occasions. However, absent unprecedented and credible access to the minds of past Soviet leaders—in most cases now difficult—the actual value and role of U.S. Cold War deterrence policies will continue to be an open question.[4] Even as some

---

2. For the most comprehensive presentation of the thesis that deterrence of a U.S.-Soviet conflict was solid without the U.S. nuclear threat, see John Mueller, *Retreat from Doomsday: The Obsolescence of Major War* (New York: Basic Books, 1989). Following an unprecedented analysis involving interviews with former Soviet officials, Richard Ned Lebow and Janice Gross Stein conclude on this point that, "with the benefit of hindsight, it is apparent that although both superpowers hoped to remake the world in their image, neither Moscow nor Washington was ever so dissatisfied with the status quo that it was tempted to go to war to force a change. It was not only the absence of opportunity that kept the peace, but also the absence of a strong motive for war." *We All Lost the Cold War* (Princeton: Princeton Univ. Press, 1995), 357.

3. As Lebow and Stein rightly note, "To identify a case of immediate deterrence success, evidence about the intentions and subsequent calculations of the would-be challenger is essential. They cannot be inferred from prior threats or *a priori* assumptions about the initiator's foreign policy." Richard Ned Lebow and Janice Gross Stein, *When Does Deterrence Succeed and How Do We Know?* (Ottawa, Ontario: Canadian Institute for International Peace and Security, 1990), 58. Gordon Craig and Alexander George observe, "Nuclear deterrence strategy has been the subject of numerous critical assessments, all of them hampered by lack of good data on the impact that nuclear threats have had on intended targets." *Force and Statecraft: Diplomatic Problems of Our Time*, 3d ed. (New York: Oxford Univ. Press, 1995), 195.

4. Even following their analysis of Soviet and U.S. decision-making concerning the Cuban missile crisis and the 1973 Yom Kippur war, Lebow and Stein conclude that lessons concerning the role of nuclear deterrence threats "must remain tentative until additional evidence becomes available about other critical confrontations during the Cold War and about the role of nuclear weapons in Sino-American and Sino-Soviet relations." *We All Lost the Cold War*, 364. Clearly, conclusions may remain tentative for a very long time.

snippets of Soviet Cold War decision-making become visible,[5] it is implausible to anticipate that a sufficient base of evidence soon will be available to demonstrate that it was in fact U.S. nuclear deterrence policies that prevented Soviet attack throughout the Cold War. The past Soviet penchant to adjust history to comport with political expediency may complicate this problem for future research.

There is no doubt that policies of deterrence can "work." It is, however, difficult to produce evidence "proving" that a policy of deterrence led an opponent to reject some provocation that it otherwise would have undertaken. Opposing leaders frequently are not generous in explaining or documenting why they did not attack on any given occasion when they otherwise were planning to do so. Unfortunately, the relative lack of evidence on this matter is no impediment to those, including senior U.S. government and military leaders, who claim, with apparent certainty, that the U.S. effectively deterred Soviet attack throughout the Cold War. The Department of Defense's 1996 annual report claims, for example, that following the Second World War, "the United States concentrated on the second line of defense—deterrence. Over the next 40-plus years, deterrence worked and World War III was averted."[6] It is comforting to so conclude that the Soviet Union was deterred by our carefully crafted and elaborate policies of deterrence. Such a conclusion suggests great sophistication in our formulation and implementation of nuclear deterrence policy, that America's "best and brightest" knew what they were doing with regard to deterrence and nuclear weapons, and that they and their successors will be able to design future policies with confidence based on past success. Much less comforting is the possibility that our knowledge of how to deter *in practice* is limited, that our past policies are suspect for the future, and that there is much about deter-

5. Some very interesting initial work in this area is beginning to surface, in particular, Lebow and Stein, *We All Lost the Cold War*. A remarkable work regarding Soviet arms control decision-making by a Russian academic working with a retired Russian general is Aleksandr Savelyev and Nikolay Detinov, *The Big Five: Arms Control Decision-Making in the Soviet Union* (Westport, Conn.: Praeger, 1995). See also Aleksandr Savelyev and Nikolay Detinov, "The Krasnoyarsk Affair," *Comparative Strategy* 12, no. 3 (July–September 1993): 343–50.

6. See William J. Perry, *Annual Report to the President and the Congress* (Washington, D.C.: GPO, March 1996), iv.

ring in the second nuclear age that is, and is likely to remain, understood only dimly.

The question that now challenges us is whether the deterrence theory and policies that so dominated the Cold War can provide useful guidance for U.S. policy in the second nuclear age, when protagonists are likely to be WMD-armed regional aggressors asserting their power locally (as was the case with Iraq in the Gulf war). Can the United States deter regional powers from provocations, including their use of WMD? And are past approaches to deterrence likely to be useful?

Deterrence Old Think

Since the collapse of the Soviet Union and the bipolar system, there has been little reconsideration of past deterrence theory or policies for their relevance to the second nuclear age.[7] Rather, there has been a widespread obliviousness to possible problems with accepted wisdom and policies. This reluctance appears to be based on a belief that U.S. Cold War nuclear deterrence theory and policies worked well for more than four decades, so why should they be questioned now? Why should past policies not also work against the prospective foes of the second nuclear age? As the old aphorism goes, "If it ain't broke, don't fix it."

Yet, did we really learn "how to deter" during the Cold War? Is Sir Michael Howard correct, for example, when he states emphatically that "it is beyond doubt," that we "effectively deterred the Soviet Union from using military force to achieve its political objectives" and that "we have become rather expert at deterrence"?[8] Or do confident statements of deterrence effectiveness and our expertise in applying deterrence policies simply reflect the fact that the Soviet behavior we saw was what we hoped our

---

7. As Fred C. Iklé has observed with regard to the Pentagon's 1994 Nuclear Posture Review, "The Pentagon, after spending a year to study U.S. nuclear strategy, discovered a 'requirement' of 3500 warheads, based on the Cold War calculus of Mutual Assured Destruction." "Facing Nuclear Reality," *Wall Street Journal*, 2 January 1996, 8. While the Pentagon's effort had little hope of any serious reconsideration of "old think," an excellent initial reassessment is Paul Davis and John Arquilla, *Deterring or Coercing Opponents in Crisis* (Santa Monica, Calif.: RAND, 1991).

8. Sir Michael Howard, "Lessons of the Cold War," *Survival* 36, no. 4 (winter 1994–95): 161, 164.

deterrence polices would accomplish, not always their actual effect? Did our deterrence policies, for example, seek to prevent a military onslaught that Soviet leaders never seriously contemplated or rejected for reasons independent of our nuclear deterrence efforts? The record is not yet available for definitive conclusions to be drawn, and may never be so.

Nevertheless, there are frequent definitive expressions of confidence on this issue by senior U.S. government officials, military leaders and prominent commentators. For example, Jan Lodal, Principal Deputy Undersecretary of Defense for Policy, claimed in July 1995 that "nuclear deterrence worked throughout the Cold War, it continues to work now, it will work into the future. . . . The exact same kinds of nuclear deterrence calculations that have always worked will continue to work."[9]

Such confident claims about the past and future of deterrence are not unusual. Joseph Nye, an Assistant Secretary of Defense for International Security Affairs, recently observed, "If deterrence prevented 10,000 Soviet missiles from reaching the United States, it baffles me as to why it wouldn't prevent 20 Chinese missiles from reaching Alaska." Nye continues by observing, with apparent certainty, "I know how to deter" a Chinese missile threat.[10] Then-Deputy Secretary of Defense John Deutch stated in

---

9. Jan Lodal (P)DUSD, Ashton Carter ASD (International Security Policy), with selected reporters, 31 July 1995, Washington, D.C., News Conference Transcript, 9–10 (mimeographed). There are numerous expressions of confidence from Capitol Hill that Cold War notions of deterrence stability should continue to guide U.S. policy. See, for example, the statements by Senator John Kerry in Senate Committee on Foreign Relations, *Administration's Proposal to Seek Modification of the 1972 Anti-Ballistic Missile Treaty*, 10 March 1994, 38–44 (transcript).

10. From remarks to the Defense Writers Group, 18 October 1995, Washington, D.C., quoted in, "Word for Word," *Defense News*, 23–29 October 1995, 26. It should be noted in this regard that in 1995, while in Beijing, Nye was asked by Chinese officials how the United States would respond if Taiwan were threatened. According to Secretary of Defense Perry, Nye's reply was: "We don't know what we would do, and you don't—because it's going to depend on the circumstances, and you don't know what we would do." After relating Nye's response to the Chinese officials in Beijing, Perry added, "I do not believe we will make a statement more definite than that." This obvious intentional ambiguity by Nye and Perry might help to deter a risk-adverse challenger; it also could help lead a risk-tolerant adversary to perceive a weakness of U.S. commitment as an opening to be exploited. Whether the Chinese leadership will prove to be risk-tolerant or risk-adverse on the issue of Taiwan remains to be seen. See *Remarks by Secretary of Defense William Perry at Washington Institute for Near East Policy*, Washington, D.C., 6 February 1996, transcript by Federal News Service; see also, "Perry Voices Concern for Taiwan," *New York Times*, 7 February 1996, A3; "World-Wide," *Wall Street Journal*, 7 February 1996, 1; and, "Pentagon: China asked about Taiwan Clash," *Washington Times*, 15 December 1995, A22.

congressional testimony that "deterrence is *ensured* by having a survivable [nuclear] capability to hold at risk what potentially hostile leaders value, and we will maintain that capability."[11] And the most recent Department of Defense annual report continues this refrain: "Strategic [nuclear] forces remain a critical element of the U.S. policy of deterrence. Although these forces are being reduced in the aftermath of the Cold War, and the percentage of the defense budget devoted to them is declining, strategic forces will continue to provide a strong and credible deterrent to nuclear attack."[12]

Such confidence is not by any means restricted to the current crop of Pentagon officials; it is long-standing and thoroughly bipartisan. Dick Cheney's 1993 *Annual Report of the Secretary of Defense to the President and the Congress* asserts confidently that a "strong U.S nuclear force provides a secure retaliatory capability that serves to deter the use of weapons of mass destruction while providing unambiguous warning to potential aggressors who have acquired these capabilities or are in the process of acquiring them."[13]

This widely expressed belief that deterrence, in the words of Deutch, is "ensured" by a severe nuclear threat, also is sounded by prominent commentator John Pike of the Federation of American Scientists: "I am assuming that deterrence will work with these [rogue] countries as it worked with Josef Stalin and Chairman Mao: 'We'll turn you into a sea of radioactive glass 20 minutes later.'"[14] Spurgeon Keeny, executive director of the Arms

---

11. John Deutch, testimony in U.S. House, Committee on Foreign Affairs, *U.S. Nuclear Policy: Hearings*, 103d Cong., 2d sess. (Washington, D.C.: GPO, 1995), 36 (my emphasis).

12. Perry, *Annual Report to the President and the Congress*, 218.

13. Secretary of Defense Dick Cheney, *Report of the Secretary of Defense to the President and the Congress* (Washington, D.C.: GPO, January 1993), 67.

14. Quoted in Rowan Scarborough, "It's Not 'Star Wars II,' Republicans Say in Fighting for Missile Defense," *Washington Times*, 23 January 1995, A1, A9. "TRB" of the *New Republic* makes essentially the same prosaic assertion, that deterrence "worked just fine" against the Soviet Union and will work vis-à-vis rogue states because their leaders know that they "would be squashed like a bug upon emerging [from their bunkers]." "Crazy State," *New Republic* (5 December 1994): 6. As another journalist graphically put it, "Can anybody truly imagine Iraq or Syria launching a missile attack against American soil— knowing that we would still have, even after massive reductions in strategic arms, enough missiles to erase them from the map?" Richard Matthews, "Air Force Strange New Argument for 'Star Wars,'" *Atlanta Journal*, 16 January 1990, 14.

Control Association, when commenting on the future deterrence of regional rogue states, expressed extreme confidence in deterrence policies and his own understanding of deterrence by claiming to know that "even fanatical, paranoid regimes are deterred by the prospect of catastrophic consequences."[15] Similarly, Ambassador Jonathan Dean, advisor to the Union of Concerned Scientists, claims with unfettered certainty that, "Deterrence is not just a theory. It is validated by evidence from real life, including the forty years of mutual Cold War nuclear standoff between the United States and the Soviet Union. Nor does it apply only to large, nuclear armed states. . . . Deterrence will remain a reliable defense against possible rogue missile attack on the United States [because] they know their regimes would be wiped out if they actually launched a missile attack on the United States."[16]

Confidence in the reliability of deterrence based on U.S. threats of nuclear retaliation is reflected also in Congressional discussions of the subject. For example, Congressman Ronald Dellums, the well-informed and articulate former chairman of the House of Representatives' Armed Services Committee, indicated his confidence in nuclear deterrence, stating that rogue states certainly will be deterred from striking America by the knowledge that "within hours there would be a hole in the ocean."[17] Similarly, Congressman Norm Dicks, of the House's Defense Appropriations Subcommittee, when asked about limited WMD threats to the United States responded rhetorically, "Someone would launch a single nuclear weapon at the United States? That would be the end of their country. Trident submarines, land-based missiles and B-2 bombers are the real deterrent."[18]

These expressions by senior U.S. officials and commentators about deterrence theory and practice are common. They reflect a widely held view that we can answer the question of how to deter

---

15. Spurgeon Keeny, "Inventing an Enemy," *New York Times*, 18 June 1994, 21.

16. See "The Front Lines of Defense: Prevention, Part A: Deterrence and Diplomacy," in *The Last 15 Minutes*, ed. Joseph Cirincione and Frank von Hippel (Washington, D.C.: Coalition to Reduce Nuclear Dangers, 1996), 24–25.

17. U.S. House, Committee on National Security, *Long-Range Missile Threat to the United States and Ballistic Missile Defense: Hearings*, 28 February 1996, (my transcript).

18. Quoted in "One On One," *Defense News*, 22–28 April 1996, 54.

over a broad range of prospective opponents with a confidence born from decades of successfully deterring the Soviet Union. The answer, typically, is that deterrence ultimately is "ensured" by retaliatory nuclear threats.

From the 1960s until the end of the Cold War it was accepted wisdom that we knew how to deter the Soviet Union. Indeed, so certain have U.S. officials and expert commentators appeared to be in their understanding of deterrence, that they have often felt free to claim with confidence that they could calculate with some precision how "stable" was the U.S.-Soviet deterrence relationship. Indeed, they have frequently predicted with confidence how deterrence would be affected by some prospective change in U.S. and/or Soviet strategic capabilities. For example, Nye, in company with prominent commentators Graham Allison and Albert Carnesale, expressed certainty with regard to the reliability of the U.S-Soviet nuclear deterrence relationship: "In U.S.-Soviet relations, the current nuclear postures have substantially solved the problem of deterring deliberate nuclear attack."[19] Similarly, Ashton Carter (now an assistant secretary of defense), William Perry (now secretary of defense), and John Steinbruner expressed confidence that "core deterrence" has become "securely established" and that "virtually all plausible varieties of deterrence of such deliberate attack could be underwritten with a fraction of the existing nuclear arsenals."[20]

Senior U.S. officials and expert commentators, have claimed quite a detailed understanding not only of how nuclear deterrence will operate, but how particular types of conventional forces in the U.S. arsenal will contribute to the deterrence of regional foes: "This new [advanced U.S.] conventional military capability adds a powerful dimension to the ability of the United States to deter war. While it is certainly not as powerful as nuclear weapons, it is a more credible deterrent, particularly in regional conflicts vital to U.S. national interests. . . . The new [conventional] military capa-

---

19.   "Defusing the Nuclear Menace," *Washington Post,* 4 September 1988, C1, C2.

20.   *A New Concept of Cooperative Security* (Washington, D.C.: Brookings Institution, 1992), 1.

bility can also serve as a credible deterrent to a regional power's use of chemical weapons."[21]

Confident claims to knowledge about deterrence in general and in detail are common in U.S. discussions of the subject. In fact, they typically pass without raising an eyebrow. When uttered by a senior official, all heads in attendance nod in agreement. Nevertheless, upon reflection, it should be recognized that such claims reflect considerable hubris with regard to their understanding of how to deter. The above statement, for example, lays claim to knowing that advanced U.S. conventional forces (1) will strengthen the U.S. ability to deter, (2) will pose a more credible regional deterrent threat than nuclear weapons, and (3) can pose a credible deterrent threat specifically against a regional foe's use of chemical weapons.

Generalized claims to knowledge about deterrence and its future operation, as reflected in the many statements noted above, should be recognized as well beyond what the evidence can bear. Understanding the context and the opponent is key to establishing policies of deterrence that can affect the opponent in predictable ways. This is a point reached by virtually every empirical analysis of deterrence application—as opposed to deductive and abstract deterrence theory. As Gordon Craig and Alexander George observe:

> Inherent in the calculus of deterrence lies the assumption of a rational opponent, one who can be deterred from a given course of action if the costs of pursuing it clearly outweigh the benefits to be gained thereby. While it is not the purpose here to explore all the ramifications of this assumption, it can be said that in making it, a grave and often fatal error may be committed. Not all actors in international politics calculate utility in making decisions in the same way. Differences in values, culture, attitudes toward risk-taking, and so on vary greatly. There is no substitute for knowledge of the adversary's mind-set and behavioral

21. William Perry, "Desert Storm and Deterrence," *Foreign Affairs* 70, no. 4 (Fall 1991): 66.

style, and this is often difficult to obtain or to apply correctly in assessing intentions or *predicting responses*.[22]

Nonetheless, confident statements about future U.S. deterrence effectiveness are expressed without knowing who the opponent is, whether the opponent is risk-tolerant or risk-adverse,
what the context of the assumed conflict or crisis is, how the opponent calculates the potential cost of *inaction* on its part, what the
stakes involved are, what the domestic political condition of the
opponent is, what credibility the opponent attaches to our deterrent threat, or anything other than the type of forces available to
the U.S. leader. In the numerous statements quoted above, claim is
laid to knowledge of the certain effectiveness of future U.S. deterrence policies vis-à-vis the variety of potential rogue challengers—
to the extent of asserting that nuclear deterrence is certain to be reliable even against "fanatical" and "paranoid regimes." Such zeal-
ous professions at this point represent merely the valor of ignorance.

Unless one knows how the opponent makes decisions, what
factors that particular opponent will take into account in its decision-making and how they will be weighted, such confident
statements are simply unjustified. We may speculate that, in principle and all other things being equal, a particular military balance
or capability should, under plausible conditions, predictably affect
a well-informed and sensible opponent's decision-making in a
particular manner. In practice, however, all other things frequently are not equal and opponents do not behave sensibly. The
opponent's decision-making may be driven by factors that are either unknown or underappreciated, including factors other than
the military balance or the particular U.S. capability that is expected to affect deterrence predictably.[23] The specific U.S. capability that we believe should, *in principle*, shape a generically sensible

---

22. Craig and George, *Force and Statecraft*, 188 (my emphasis). For a useful discussion
of how regime-type, for example, is likely to affect deterrence decision-making, see
Kenneth Watman and Dean Wilkening, *U.S. Regional Deterrence Strategies* (Santa Monica,
Calif.: RAND, 1995), 27–55.

23. According to the assessment by Lebow and Stein, during both the Cuban missile
crisis and the nuclear alert crisis of the Yom Kippur war, neither U.S. nor Soviet leaders
were driven by close calculations of the strategic balance in their decision-making. See
Lebow and Stein, *We All Lost the Cold War*, 359–68.

opponent's decision-making in a particular direction may actually be irrelevant or of only modest significance. In the absence of knowledge about the opponent and the context—which is the case by definition in sweeping statements about the future effectiveness of deterrence policies and forces—grandiose and confident claims can be based on little more than how we believe an opponent "should" behave if it is as rational and sensible as we suppose. Little certainty can be attached to any such prediction.

It is ironic that leaders and commentators, often with deserved and impressive scientific and technical credentials, frequently make sweeping and confident claims about deterrence, with little or no supporting evidence. They would likely never make similarly definitive statements, with so little basis, on a technical question; yet with questions of deterrence, such claims are and have long been the norm. In the past, those lobbying against nuclear modernization have usually claimed knowledge that deterrence would remain stable even if the U.S. nuclear arsenal were frozen or severely reduced—as if they truly knew how to deter so well that they could confidently predict how specific adjustments to the nuclear arsenal would affect the U.S.-Soviet deterrence relationship. Former senior officials McGeorge Bundy and William Crowe Jr. and noted scientist Sidney Drell express definitive knowledge that "it simply is not true that smaller plans with smaller forces will be inadequate for strategic deterrence. The possibility of even a few nuclear detonations in populated areas provides ample deterrence."[24] There is, it must be noted, virtually no evidence on which to base such a claim, unbound as it is by time or context.

Nevertheless, commentators and officials frequently make similar claims of knowledge concerning the deterrence of nuclear strikes against the United States or its allies by *any* opponent, clearly assuming a generically-sensible foe. For example, in 1991 Carl Kaysen, Robert McNamara, and George Rathjens claimed that "the United States can dispense with modernizing the remaining [nuclear] weapons. They are already efficacious enough to serve the residual function of minimum deterrence of the use of

---

24. McGeorge Bundy, William J. Crowe Jr., and Sidney Drell, *Reducing Nuclear Danger* (New York: Council on Foreign Relations Press, 1993), 95.

nuclear weapons by *any state* against the United States or its allies."[25]

These and many comparable statements by senior officials and commentators clearly reflect confidence in their belief that they know how to deter under existing and hypothetical conditions, and thus can predict how deterrence will function in the future— even to the point of expressing no doubt that deterrence will function with "a fraction" of the existing nuclear force, or that the "possibility of even a few nuclear detonations will provide ample deterrence."

The prevalence of this apparent confidence at official and expert levels has reached down to most popular journalistic discussions of the subject. Citing a recent academic study, the author of a *New York Times* article repeats the common fallacy of claiming to know that "nuclear deterrence has worked for a half century," and then goes on to charge that the United States wasted vast amounts of money by buying far too many nuclear weapons.[26] Yet, unless one knows just how much nuclear threat was necessary to deter Soviet leaders at critical decision points throughout the Cold War, how can one claim with authority that the United States purchased far too much nuclear capability? Perhaps the United States did overbuild, perhaps not; there is yet precious little on which to draw such conclusions. This is not to say that confident statements about deterrence are certain to be incorrect; the point is that there are virtually no grounds, other than intuition or hope, for making sweeping claims about the effectiveness of nuclear deterrence throughout the Cold War, or to predict how future challengers will behave in response to familiar deterrence policies under various hypothetical conditions.

Cold War arms control agreements with the Soviet Union typically were based on the expectation that the United States could predictably strengthen deterrence stability by shaping the U.S. and Soviet strategic capabilities in a particular direction. This, of course, presupposed that we understood deterrence and the op-

25.   Carl Kaysen, Robert McNamara, and George Rathjens, "Nuclear Weapons after the Cold War," *Foreign Affairs* 70, no. 4 (Fall 1991): 108 (my emphasis).

26.   Peter Passell, "Economic Scene: A Lot of Money Spent on Nuclear Arms Was Wasted, a Study Shows," *New York Times*, 14 December 1995, D2.

ponent so well that we knew how particular forces would affect deterrence stability. That we were so knowledgeable was accepted widely for decades, and the United States constructed arms control policies on the basis of that supposed knowledge. Stanley Riveles, a current senior official at the U.S. Arms Control and Disarmament Agency, has observed that the 1972 ABM Treaty limiting missile defense systems "is the bedrock of strategic stability,"[27] and that the treaty's "primary contribution" has been in "maintaining strategic stability."[28] Similarly, Strobe Talbott, now deputy secretary of state, claims as if it were a law of physics that by so limiting missile defenses the United States and the Soviet Union "were decreasing the chances that they would attack each other."[29] The preamble to the ABM Treaty itself claims that limits on strategic missile defense "would lead to a decrease in the risk of outbreak of war involving nuclear weapons." The presumption, of course, is that we know that structuring U.S. and Soviet forces in accordance with the treaty (that is, rejecting missile defenses) affected U.S. and Soviet decision-making in such a way as to strengthen deterrence and thereby reduce the probability of nuclear war.

The penchant for claiming knowledge of how arms control agreements would affect U.S.-Soviet (now U.S.-Russian) deterrence relations has been extended to the initial agreements of the second nuclear age. In December 1995 the U.S. Senate agreed to make no changes to the START II Treaty, signed by Presidents Bush and Yeltsin in 1991. In his summary argument for the treaty Senator Richard Lugar, a main sponsor in the Senate, described it as "a substantial step forward to strategic stability."[30]

The penchant for claiming knowledge of deterrence theory and practice (how to create "stability") is pervasive across the

---

27. Stanley Riveles, acting commissioner, U.S. Standing Consultative Commission, *Address to the Seventh Multinational Conference on Theater Missile Defense*, 21 June 1994, 1 (mimeographed).

28. Stanley Riveles, "Continuity and Change in ABM Treaty Policy," remarks delivered to the Eighth Multinational Conference on Theater Missile Defense, London, printed in U.S. Arms Control And Disarmament Agency, *Arms Control Text*, 6 June 1995, 1.

29. Strobe Talbott, *Endgame: The Inside Story of SALT II* (New York: Harper and Row, 1979), 22.

30. Quoted in "Senate Debates START Treaty," *Washington Times*, 24 December 1995, A2.

entire political spectrum. In the early to mid-1980s, for example, proponents of the large, accurate, and multi-warheaded MX ICBM claimed with apparent certainty that U.S. deployment of one hundred MX missiles was critical for continued deterrence stability. It was argued that the MX would redress the Soviet advantage in the capability to threaten hardened military targets, and that redressing that advantage was important for deterrence stability. As President Reagan's 1983 Commission on Strategic Forces, headed by Brent Scowcroft, claimed, "Effective deterrence of any Soviet temptation to threaten or launch a massive conventional or a limited nuclear war thus requires us to have a comparable ability to destroy Soviet military targets. . . . A one-sided strategic condition in which the Soviet Union could effectively destroy the whole range of strategic targets in the United States, but we could not effectively destroy a similar range of targets in the Soviet Union, would be extremely unstable over the long run."[31] Here we were told with confidence that without missiles of a specific type to create a symmetry of a specific type in U.S. and Soviet strategic nuclear capabilities, deterrence would become "extremely unstable." Perhaps stability really did require the MX (although only half the force recommended by Scowcroft was ever deployed), perhaps not: there was very little ground other than "gut feelings" for claiming with such precision what would constitute a stable U.S.-Soviet nuclear balance in practice and over time.

Clearly, if widely accepted propositions about deterrence have considerable supporting empirical evidence and a long history of apparent success, they should not be challenged lightly. As we have seen, however, limited empirical evidence is available—the extended period of peace in U.S.-Soviet relations proves little in this regard. We simply do not know with such certainty why Soviet leaders did not do what they did not do. (It should be recalled in this regard that there was a similarly long period of general peace in Europe following the 1871 Franco-Prussian War, until the dramatic outbreak of world war in 1914.) The duration of the peace of the Cold War, in and of itself, demonstrates only that

---

31. President's Commission on Strategic Forces, *Report of the President's Commission on Strategic Forces* (Washington, D.C.: Department of Defense, 6 April 1983), 6.

U.S. policies of deterrence did not demonstrably fail, not that they were effective. The distinction here between not failing and working effectively is not merely a matter of semantics. A bridge engineered to accommodate 60-ton loads may hold up for decades under the relatively stress-free environment of constant 4-ton loads. This record does not demonstrate that the bridge performed to its design for decades, or that it will do so in the future. It simply demonstrates that the bridge did not fail for decades; the first 60-ton load will be the real test. Similarly, ample questions remain as to how well or if our deterrence policies performed under serious tests, we simply know that they never failed.[32]

I do not mean here to be critical of particular officials and commentators whose hubris about deterrence has been accepted and standard fare throughout the broad "defense intellectual community" for decades. A generation of defense officials and intellectuals has simply persuaded itself that it "knows deterrence" with a very high degree of certainty and that deterrence stability can be manipulated with predictable reliability.[33] This conclusion does not take out of context the various expressions of confidence in deterrence, past and future. Neither is it a straw man. Such certainty, with few exceptions, permeates past and present official and expert discussions of deterrence. On the basis of past confidence, the United States shaped its Cold War force requirements and arms control policies. Now, it is finding expression in claims by senior officials and commentators that the same general approach to deterrence policy will provide the basis for the reliable deterrence of regional foes in the second nuclear age. Yet, if we cannot be certain of the functioning of nuclear deter-

---

32. Fred Iklé, a former senior Pentagon official and director of the Arms Control and Disarmament Agency, has made the intriguing point that on several occasions, "still largely shrouded in secrecy," accidents and mistakes brought the superpowers "just short of the abyss," and that on these occasions "the world escaped nuclear holocaust—seemingly by accident." Iklé, "Second Coming of the Nuclear Age," 127.

33. There are, of course, exceptions. Several more cautious senior officials and prominent commentators appear never to have accepted the prevalent opinion that deterrence had become so well understood that it could be manipulated so predictably. See, for example, Fred Charles Iklé, "Nuclear Strategy: Can There Be a Happy Ending?" *Foreign Affairs* 63, no. 4 (spring 1985): 810–26; Iklé, "Can Nuclear Deterrence Last Out the Century," *Foreign Affairs* 51, no. 2 (January 1973): 267–85; and Iklé, "Second Coming of the Nuclear Age." It should be noted that strong expressions of concern about our ability to predict and manipulate deterrence stability have been considered iconoclastic within the defense community.

rence in the past, how much less credible are the claims that it will work in the future, when conditions have so changed?

Perhaps some of the officials cited above, in fact, appreciate the limitations of deterrence more than is reflected in their various statements—statements which may have been uttered for political effect or as short-hand. The problem, of course, is that confident expressions by those who may know better are adopted over time as axioms by commentators, legislators, and other officials who, unschooled in the subject, understandably do not appreciate the need for nuance and caution when extolling the certainty that deterrence will "work."

The Risk of Overconfidence

The high degree of confidence that officials and commentators have in their Cold War-inspired knowledge of how to deter poses a risk to national security in the second nuclear age. Indeed, there are several reasons why it presents the potential for real danger. U.S. Cold War nuclear deterrence policy included general expectations that opponents would behave sensibly and that their behavior would be affected strongly and predictably by the character of the strategic nuclear balance. This expectation is, in part, consistent with deterrence theory, which is predicated on the assumption of an opponent rationally weighing the potential costs and benefits of its behavior. Yet, "sensible" behavior frequently is in the eye of the beholder and dependent on the character of the opponent and the context of the engagement. It is difficult to step outside one's own frame of reference to understand that others may have very different interpretations of what is sensible and reasonable and may calculate costs and gains differently. The assumption of a reasonable opponent can lead to mistaken expectations of the opponent's behavior and costly surprises.

I distinguish here between being "rational" and being "sensible" or "reasonable." Rational refers to a method of decision-making: taking in information, prioritizing values, conceptualizing various options, and choosing the course of action that maximizes value. In contrast, sensible refers to whether one is perceived as behaving in ways that are understandable to the observer, and may therefore be anticipated. This may involve having goals, a value hierarchy, and behavior patterns that, if not shared, are familiar to the observers. One can be quite rational within one's own decision-making framework, yet grossly outside the observer's understanding or norm. One can be quite rational within one's own framework of values, but be viewed as unreasonable and not sensible by an opponent. Saddam Hussein, for example, probably is a rational decision-maker, but in 1990–91 he was far from sensible or reasonable by Washington's standards because he was surprisingly risk-tolerant. I find this contrast helpful for distinguishing between behavior that is rational but nonetheless surprising, and "sensible" behavior that can easily be anticipated because it fits within a familiar frame of reference.

Western leaders, working from a deterrence framework and banking on their opponents being generically sensible and rational, have been surprised in the past by opponents who held to an alternative interpretation of sensible behavior. These opponents were not deterred from provocation, even though Western officials thought they should be. The opponents' behavior, while not strictly irrational, was unexpected because it was outside the bounds of what was considered sensible by Western leaders, who misjudged their opponents, were surprised by their aggression, and paid the price of their own mistaken expectations.

A striking example may be seen in Prime Minister Neville Chamberlain's behavior leading up to World War II. "The lesson of Munich" should caution against acceptance of a fundamental assumption of U.S. Cold War deterrence policy, that prospective opponents will behave in sensible, predictable ways. Chamberlain assumed, against much evidence, that Hitler would be "reasonable" and that his objective was "justice" for Germany and the *deutsches Volk* in Czechoslovakia. Convinced that Hitler would not permit, much less kindle, another world conflagration, and limited by self-inflicted military weakness, Chamberlain went to Munich to parlay with Hitler with few, if any, acceptable alternatives to appeasement.[34] This combination was a recipe for the

---

34. For a review of Chamberlain's role in the military weakness that constrained Britain, see Telford Taylor, *Munich: The Price of Peace* (New York: Vintage Books, 1979), 212–14, 588–90.

failure of what now is called "crisis management." As Winston Churchill repeatedly observed of Chamberlain's appeasement policy, "You were given the choice between war and dishonour. You chose dishonour and you shall have war."

One of the widely cited reasons for Chamberlain's policy of appeasement was the fear he shared with much of the British political elite that war with Germany could result in the rapid destruction of European civilization. Long-range air power was thought to have made war unthinkable; it *had* to be avoided. Official British estimates of likely bombing casualties were grossly exaggerated. They were believed at the time, however, and had a paralyzing effect on British willingness to challenge Hitler[35] or take actions that might provoke the *Führer*.

The story of appeasement at Munich illustrates well the danger of Neville Chamberlain's assumption that Hitler, ultimately, would be sensible (as defined in London). Chamberlain's reassuring assumption about Hitler led to mistaken expectations about the *Führer's* likely behavior. Chamberlain continued to believe, against much contrary evidence, that Hitler too appreciated that another general war *had* to be avoided, that if only they could sit down and discuss German concerns, Hitler, as a sensible leader, would come to a settlement short of war.

But Hitler's views were fundamentally incompatible with those of Chamberlain and the British appeasers. As Williamson Murray notes, "The problem was that Hitler did not want a settlement; he wanted a limited war with Czechoslovakia."[36] Nevertheless, the hope that reason would prevail led the British government to refuse to see the probability of war until after the occupation of Prague in March 1939.[37] In this case, the assumption was that Hitler shared the general British view, and certainly Chamberlain's view, that extreme provocations likely to lead to

35. See the discussion in Fredrick Sallagar, *The Road to Total War* (New York: Van Nostrand Reinhold, 1969), 15; Barry R. Posen, *The Sources of Military Doctrine* (Ithaca: Cornell Univ. Press, 1984), 145–46; and J.M. Spaight, *Air Power in the Next War* (London: Geoffrey Bles, 1938), 126.

36. Williamson Murray, "Munich at Fifty," *Commentary* (July 1988): 57.

37. See Brian Bond and Williamson Murray, "The British Armed Forces, 1918–1939," in *Military Effectiveness*, vol. 2, *The Interwar Period*, ed. Allan R. Millett and Williamson Murray (Boston: Allan and Unwin, 1988), 109.

another European conflagration had to be avoided. Chamberlain built his policy of appeasement upon this misjudgment of Hitler, that he would be similarly constrained by the prospect of war. Although Hitler may not have sought another general European war, he was quite willing to pursue provocations judged as beyond reason in London.

Another World War II example further illustrates the danger involved in believing that one can predict how the opponent defines reasonable behavior. The following quotations are most instructive. At roughly the point when Prime Minister Tojo Hideki told the Japanese emperor, "Our empire has no alternative but to begin war," Assistant Secretary of State Acheson was advising the president persuasively that war was unlikely because "no rational Japanese could believe an attack on us could result in anything but disaster for his country."[38] As Acheson's statement suggests, the U.S. policy of attempting to coerce the Japanese out of China via an oil embargo was based on an assumption that the Japanese leadership would concede to U.S. demands rather than risk battle with a foe whose economic and military potential was so much greater than its own.[39] Clearly Acheson's expectations were only half right: the attack on Pearl Harbor did ultimately bring disaster to Japan, but Japanese leaders nevertheless ordered the attack. The U.S. effort to coerce Japan out of China instead channeled the Japanese to the surprise attack on Pearl Harbor.

A final recent example will suffice here. Prior to the 1990 Iraqi invasion of Kuwait, various intelligence assessments reportedly warned the Bush administration that Iraq appeared to be preparing to invade. Senior officials, however, were unpersuaded, largely because they had judged Saddam to be a rational and sensible decision-maker and, from their perspective, an Iraqi decision to invade Kuwait was not sensible.[40] In a telling statement, the former U.S. ambassador to Iraq, April Glaspie,

---

38. Quoted in Scott Sagan, "The Origins of the Pacific War," *Journal of Interdisciplinary History* 18, no. 4 (Spring 1988): 894, 906.

39. See the discussion in Alexander George, *Forceful Persuasion* (Washington, D.C.: U.S. Institute of Peace, 1991): 19–23.

40. See Alex Hybel, *Power over Rationality* (Albany: State Univ. of New York Press, 1993), 51–56.

stated that Saddam's behavior was unexpected because "we overestimated Saddam Hussein's instinct for self-preservation."[41]

Despite an abundance of intelligence pointing to an invasion, U.S. leaders were surprised. Senior Bush administration officials "assumed that Saddam would not invade Kuwait because he was a rational actor and had learned from Iraq's war with Iran how costly another major war would be." They "held fast to this belief even after they had been warned by the Defense Intelligence Agency and Central Intelligence Agency that Iraq was getting ready to attack Kuwait. . . . From the beginning its [the Bush administration's] principal members assumed that Saddam would assess the benefits and costs of an invasion in a manner similar to their own. They never accounted for the possibility, even as the information they processed gained clarity, that the Iraqi leader might eye the international environment through a set of lenses quite different from theirs."[42] One analysis of U.S. expectations in the Gulf war has concluded, with obvious understatement, "All in all, the record of predicting Saddam's behavior was less than glorious."[43]

Bush administration officials could have joined with Acheson and Chamberlain in observing how unexpected and "senseless" was the opponent's ultimate behavior. That, of course, is the point: deterrence theory posits a rational, reasonable, and to a large extent predictable opponent. History demonstrates, however, that opponents often do not understand one another well and therefore behave in ways that appear "senseless"—even when each party involved believes, by its own light, that it is calculating rationally and behaving reasonably. This can lead to costly misjudgments.

These brief examples are by no means isolated.[44] They point to a significant potential problem. Expectations of a sensible oppo-

---

41. Quoted in Davis and Arquilla, *Deterring or Coercing Opponents*, 68.

42. Hybel, *Power Over Rationality*, 7, 51–52; see also George, *Forceful Persuasion*, 61–63.

43. Davis and Arquilla, *Deterring or Coercing Opponents*, v.

44. There are numerous additional historical examples of surprising behavior resulting from assumptions that proved to be mistaken about the character of a leadership. As former director of the CIA Stansfield Turner said of the Iranian revolution: "I'm the guy who lost Iran. We didn't adequately predict the fall of the Shah. One reason was that while we saw the Shah declining in popularity and influence in his country, we were unwilling to

nent are clearly a basis for the prevalent view that, just as deterrence worked throughout the Cold War, it will continue to work in the second nuclear age: sensible leaders in developing countries "won't dare" a severe provocation because we have the capability to wield nuclear retaliatory threats. As described above, U.S. officials have expressed faith in deterrence against future foes in general, without reference to the specific foe or context. This official confidence in deterrence is, of course, in keeping with the expectation of a rational, reasonable, and therefore predictable opponent.

Unfortunately, our expectations of opponents' behavior frequently are unmet, not because our opponents necessarily are irrational but because we do not understand them—their individual values, goals, determination, and commitments—in the context of the engagement, and therefore we are surprised when their "unreasonable" behavior differs from our expectations. By focusing so heavily and with such confidence on deterrence and the predictability of a generically sensible foe, U.S. leaders limit their capacity to anticipate an opponent's behavior when it falls outside their interpretation of what is reasonable. Winston Churchill's admonition, "However absorbed a commander may be in the elaboration of his own thoughts, it is sometimes necessary to take the enemy into account,"[45] is violated with some regularity.

Assuming that deterrence will "work" because the opponent will behave sensibly is bound to be the basis for a future surprise. I do not know whether our expectations of a generically sensible opponent will next be dashed by a so-called rogue state, such as North Korea, or by another challenger. That they will be dashed, however, is near certain. As we move into the second nuclear age and confront opponents with whom we are relatively unfamiliar, assumptions of a generically sensible foe almost certainly will en-

---

believe that he would not call out the troops when the crisis came and spill blood on the streets if necessary. We had pretty good data on what was happening, but we didn't make the right assumption." Statement by Stansfield Turner, *U.S. Security Interests in the 1990s*, ed. Gary Bertsch and Suzette Grillot, University of Georgia, Russell Symposium, Proceedings, 24 May 1993 (Athens: Center for East-West Trade Policy, Univ. of Georgia), 19.

45. In Robert Debs Heinl, *Dictionary of Military and Naval Quotations* (Annapolis, Md.: U.S. Naval Institute Press, 1966), 102.

sure surprises. And, as is suggested by Chamberlain's misjudgment of Hitler and the Bush administration's apparent misjudgment of Saddam Hussein, even an abundance of evidence indicating that the opponent is moving in ways we find unreasonable
may not be sufficient to overcome preconceived expectations and
prevent a costly surprise.

Fortunately, some U.S. commentators, military officers, and
senior government officials have recently begun to express reservations about assumptions of a generically sensible opponent and
their capacity to predict how deterrence will operate. The 1994
Department of Defense annual report, for example, observed that
"new proliferators might not be susceptible to basic deterrence as
practiced during the Cold War. New deterrent approaches are
needed as well as new strategies should deterrence fail."[46] Or, as
Secretary of Defense Perry observed in March 1995, "The bad
news is that in this era, deterrence may not provide even the cold
comfort it did during the Cold War. We may be facing terrorists or
rogue regimes with ballistic missiles and nuclear weapons at the
same time in the future, and they may not buy into our deterrence
theory. Indeed, they may be madder than 'MAD.'"[47]

Rethinking established theories and policies, however, is a
painful and uncertain process in any field. This may be even more
the case in national security considerations because billions of dollars, arms control treaties, the raison d'être of governmental
agencies and nongovernmental organizations, and many careers
have been built on the leitmotiv of deterrence "old think." Even

---

46. Les Aspin, *Annual Report to the President and the Congress* (Washington D.C.: GPO, January 1994), 35.

47. Secretary of Defense William J. Perry, *On Ballistic Missile Defense: Excerpt from a Speech to the Chicago Council on Foreign Relations*, 8 March 1995, 1 (mimeographed). Reservations concerning the certainty of deterrence are not limited to U.S. officials. A prominent Russian military expert, Gen. Mikhail Vinogradov, recently observed:

> The events in the Persian Gulf have shown that the presence of totalitarian regimes in certain countries, ethnic and religious strife both between the peoples of several states as well as inside them can lead and have already led to armed conflict and even war. Wars of such a nature belong to the category of unpreventable because in these cases the system of global nuclear deterrence does not work.

M.S. Vinogradov, *Report by the Coordinator of the 1st Section at the Plenary Session of the Conference on the Problems of the Global System of Protection*, 22 November 1993, Moscow, 3 (mimeographed).

when some U.S. officials indicate recognition that deterrence "old think" may not fit the second nuclear age, they typically retreat quickly to the comfort of now-traditional thought and parlance on the subject. Most recently, for example, Secretary Perry has rightly noted that U.S. nuclear and conventional capabilities "should be enough to warn off any nation from using weapons of mass destruction. But the reality is that the simple threat of retaliation may not be enough to deter some rogue nations or to deter terrorists from using these weapons. Thus we cannot always rely on deterrence."[48] This statement is heartening; it acknowledges the need to reconsider past deterrence theory and practice—at least *in the case of rogues and terrorists*.

Yet, this welcome acknowledgment of the potential fallibility of deterrence was followed promptly by confident claims that the United States "is safe" from nuclear missile attack because "deterrence has protected us from the established nuclear arsenals for decades and it will continue to protect us."[49] The proposition here is that although deterrence may be questionable in the future vis-à-vis rogues and terrorists, such as North Korea, it has held in the past and will do so in the future against "established" nuclear powers, such as, say, China.

What could be the basis for this absolute confidence in our present and future capacity to deter China, or for that matter Russia, as "established" nuclear powers? Can we know with such certainty that deterrence has and will "continue to protect us" vis-à-vis China, while there are acknowledged and very reasonable doubts about its reliability in relations with other rogues? Do we actually "know deterrence" so well that it is possible to identify with apparent certainty those states against which it will be reliable and those against which it may fail in the future? This expression of confidence and skepticism on a selective basis again reflects hubris; our understanding of deterrence theory and

48. Remarks by Defense Secretary William Perry at Georgetown University, 18 April 1996, Federal News Service, 19 April 1996, 3. See also DOD News Briefing by Secretary of Defense William J. Perry, 16 February 1996, News Briefing, Office of the Assistant Secretary of Defense (Public Affairs), 1–2.

49. Remarks Prepared for Delivery by William J. Perry, Secretary of Defense, George Washington University, 25 April 1996, News Release No. 241-96, Office of the Assistant Secretary of Defense (Public Affairs), 26 April 1996, 4.

practice is presented as so sophisticated that we can distinguish in advance those specific future cases in which deterrence will be reliable from those cases in which it may fail. Such a level of sophistication does not, in fact, exist anywhere. *If* confidence in this regard is based on the character of the current governments in Beijing and Moscow, it should be noted that the future character of those governments is very much an open question.

One can only hope that this continuing, if now selective, high level of confidence in the future of deterrence on the part of some senior officials is not tested severely, for it is based far more on hope and faith in past practice than on empirical evidence. Clearly, a fundamental reconsideration of deterrence old think, and a reorientation of policies if past concepts are found wanting, will be slow and contentious business.

The Basis for Overconfidence: Assured Vulnerability

On what basis did the U.S. defense community generally persuade itself that it understood deterrence, that it could confidently predict how deterrence might operate under varying conditions and be affected by particular arms programs and arms control policies? The answer can be found in a particular theory of strategic deterrence established by some of the most penetrating minds to address the issue following World War II.[50] This theory, the Assured Vulnerability theory of deterrence,[51] was popularized in the 1950s and 1960s, finding tremendous receptivity on Capitol Hill, among academic commentators and think tank specialists, journalists, government officials, and eventually in the military. It

---

50. For some of the brilliant, classic, early works see Albert Wohlstetter, "The Delicate Balance of Terror," *Foreign Affairs* 37, no. 2 (January 1959): 211–34; Bernard Brodie, *Strategy in the Missile Age* (Princeton: Princeton Univ. Press, 1959); Bernard Brodie, *Escalation and the Nuclear Option* (Princeton: Princeton Univ. Press, 1966); Herman Kahn, *On Thermonuclear War* (Princeton: Princeton Univ. Press, 1961); Herman Kahn, *On Escalation: Metaphors and Scenarios* (New York: Praeger, 1965); Thomas Schelling, *The Strategy of Conflict* (Cambridge: Harvard Univ. Press, 1960); Thomas Schelling, *Arms and Influence* (New Haven: Yale Univ. Press, 1966); Glen Snyder, *Deterrence and Defense: Toward a Theory of National Security* (Princeton: Princeton Univ. Press, 1961).

51. This name was first applied by Steuart Pittman, former assistant secretary of defense for civil defense. See the discussion in D.G. Brennan, "The Case for Missile Defense," *Foreign Affairs* 47, no. 3 (April 1969): 439.

became the prevailing paradigm. It involves a series of assumptions, logically related implications, and a set of policy recommendations that have significantly determined the types of forces the United States has and has not purchased, and the arms control policies it has pursued. As applied during the Cold War, its basic precept was that threats of nuclear retaliation could provide a reliable basis for deterrence. The superpowers, calculating rationally and sensibly, would refrain from extreme provocation because of the ultimate possibility of nuclear retaliation. The widespread acceptance of this general deterrence framework set the stage for the prevailing sense that deterrence could be well understood and manipulated reliably by adjusting U.S. and Soviet nuclear arsenals.[52]

Assured Vulnerability is a broad theory of deterrence and encompasses the three alternative approaches to deterrence policy that have served as the basis for Western debate on the subject: the "War-Fighting" approach, with its heavy strategic force requirements; "Minimum Deterrence," with very modest strategic force requirements; and "Mutual Assured Destruction" (usually shortened to MAD), with its requirements falling between "War-Fighting" and "Minimum Deterrence." Each of these three approaches to policy addresses the question "how much is enough" in terms of the nuclear threat thought necessary to undergird "stable" deterrence. Each was a prominent part of the Cold War debate, and together they represent a very broad spectrum of opinion on the subject.

Discussions of U.S. Cold War deterrence practice typically focused on the differences among these three different types of deterrence policy.[53] My interest is to show that, even with their differences, they fall under the same basic deterrence framework best described by the title "Assured Vulnerability." Each, for example, shares the fundamental assumption that the opponent will make

---

52. As Fred Iklé has observed, "Deterrence came to be seen as guaranteeing nonuse [of nuclear weapons], and continued nonuse as proof of successful deterrence." "Second Coming of the Nuclear Age," 123.

53. By far, the best treatment of this subject remains Colin S. Gray, *Nuclear Strategy and Strategic Planning* (Philadelphia: Foreign Policy Research Institute, 1984).

decisions based on a rational cost-benefit assessment of its prospective options. Each also assumes that

- the opponent understands at least the general character of the U.S. deterrent threat;

- U.S. strategic forces and the U.S. nuclear threat can be made sufficiently capable and credible to affect the opponent's calculation of cost and benefit predictably, and will ultimately be decisive in the opponent's decision-making;

- the opponent at least generally understands the behavior that it must avoid lest the United States execute its deterrent threat;

- the opponent controls its military forces and can prevent the provocative behavior as demanded by the United States;

- the opponent has the freedom to choose to avoid the behavior as demanded by the United States.

These shared assumptions of the War-Fighting, MAD, and Minimum Deterrence approaches to policy are, in many ways, more important than their differences. They establish an expectation about the character of the opponent and how the opponent will behave, particularly in response to the presence of a U.S. nuclear threat. Ultimately, each assumes that the opponent can be subjected to the U.S. deterrence policy, that U.S. military threats will affect the opponent's decision-making, and that the opponent will calculate that a U.S. nuclear response to its provocation would outweigh any possible benefit that could be derived from the provocation; that is, the U.S. nuclear threat, if done properly, can be decisive in shaping the opponent's choice of actions.

Three Approaches to Policy

The differences among the War-Fighting, MAD, and Minimum Deterrence approaches to policy focus on the type of nuclear threat deemed necessary for deterrence. For example, Minimum Deterrence, as the name implies, prescribes the least muscular nuclear threat. The force structure thought to be necessary and sufficient under Minimum Deterrence involves a secure retaliatory nuclear threat to destroy a relatively small number of the opponent's cities. The statement by Bundy, Crowe, and Drell cited above reflects the particular threat of Minimum Deterrence: "The possibility of even a few nuclear detonations in populated areas provides ample deterrence."[54] In short, Minimum Deterrence identifies a relatively low threshold of nuclear threat as adequate for strategic deterrence purposes.

MAD posits the need for a larger and more punishing threat to Soviet society, that being a secure retaliatory capability to inflict massive societal destruction, or "assured destruction." During the 1960s the meaning of "assured destruction" was quantified with some precision by Department of Defense analysts. Secretary McNamara, for example, identified the destruction of 20 to 25 percent of the Soviet population and 50 percent of the industrial base as sufficient for an assured destruction threat.[55] At the time, this level of threat was calculated to necessitate U.S. forces that could, "with high confidence, deliver 400 1-megaton weapons on the Soviet Union in a retaliatory strike."[56]

It should be noted that these specific Minimum Deterrence and MAD estimates of "how much is enough" were not derived from a careful examination of the opponent—how Soviet leaders calculated utility in making decisions, their values, culture, or atti-

---

54. Bundy, Crowe, and Drell, *Reducing Nuclear Danger*, 95. McGeorge Bundy's classic 1969 statement in *Foreign Affairs* best captures the ethos of Minimum Deterrence: "Think-tank analysts can set levels of 'acceptable' damage well up in the tens of millions of lives. They can assume that the loss of dozens of great cities is somehow a real choice for sane men. They are in an unreal world. In the real world of real political leaders—whether here or in the Soviet Union—a decision that would bring even one hydrogen bomb on one city of one's own country would be recognized in advance as a catastrophic blunder; ten bombs on ten cities would be a disaster beyond history; and a hundred bombs on a hundred cities are unthinkable." McGeorge Bundy, "To Cap the Volcano," *Foreign Affairs* 48, no. 1 (October 1969): 10.

55. See, for example, Alain Enthoven and Wayne K. Smith, *How Much Is Enough? Shaping the Defense Program, 1961-1969* (New York: Harper and Row, 1971), especially chaps. 5 and 6. Bernard Brodie cites one hundred Soviet cities as the sine qua non of U.S. deterrence in "The Anatomy of Deterrence," *World Politics* 11, no. 2 (January 1959): 177.

56. Enthoven and Smith, *How Much Is Enough?* 207. See also Fred Kaplan, *The Wizards of Armageddon* (Stanford: Stanford Univ. Press, 1983), 317-19.

tudes toward risk-taking. Rather, the level of threat supporting Minimum Deterrence appears to have been derived intuitively.[57] With regard to MAD, Department of Defense analysts calculated that beyond 400 secure 1-megaton weapons, the value of any additional U.S. nuclear capabilities would be limited by "strongly diminishing marginal returns."[58] The United States could double or even triple its arsenal, but this added capability would increase the level of threatened Soviet societal destruction only modestly. For MAD, once Soviet society was identified as the officially declared target of the U.S. deterrent threat, the specific requirements for deterrence were identified by a financial investment calculation.

Clearly, Minimum Deterrence and MAD are similar, differing primarily in the size of the threat thought necessary. Although Minimum Deterrence and MAD have different standards by which they judge "how much is enough," each represents a framework for limitation. That is, once the secure retaliatory threat is acquired, the requirement for deterrence under these two approaches has been met; additional nuclear capabilities are unnecessary at best and more likely represent "overkill."[59]

By the mid-1960s, the Soviet Union had acquired a sufficiently secure strategic nuclear capability to threaten U.S. cities with its own retaliatory nuclear strike. This development meant that both superpowers simultaneously possessed the nuclear retaliatory capabilities called for by Minimum Deterrence and MAD. This condition came to be seen as a "stable balance of terror" because, it was thought, given the nuclear arsenals available to each, that neither superpower could risk provoking the other to the point of general war. In theory, both sides could now safely reject calls for additional nuclear forces, for each had acquired the retaliatory forces necessary for deterrence—whether judged to be a secure

---

57. For example, Glen Snyder states, "Perhaps the most uncertain factor for the U.S. is the degree of prospective damage which would be sufficient to deter the Soviet Union from attacking. Would the Soviets be deterred by the prospect of losing ten cities? No one knows, although one might intuitively guess that the threshold is closer to ten than to two or fifty." Snyder, *Deterrence and Defense*, 57.

58. Enthoven and Smith, *How Much Is Enough?* 207.

59. See, for example, Ralph Lapp, *Kill and Overkill* (New York: Basic Books, 1962), 10, 44.

Minimum Deterrent or an "assured destruction" capability. They had acquired a "mutual sufficiency" for stable deterrence.[60] And, in fact, even if one side added to its nuclear capabilities, as long as the other retained its retaliatory threat, deterrence stability would be secure.[61]

By the late 1960s, much of the defense and foreign policy community defined "deterrence stability" in terms of mutual and secure retaliatory nuclear threats. Consequently, in the United States, those strategic systems that might to some degree serve to protect against retaliatory threats came to be regarded as "destabilizing." These systems included, in particular, ICBMs capable of threatening to destroy the opponent's retaliatory forces before they could be launched, and ballistic missile defense (BMD) that might protect cities by destroying the opponent's retaliatory forces after their launch. These "destabilizing" systems came to be seen as the enemies of deterrence stability.[62] Based on the general notion that retaliatory nuclear threats provided deterrence stability, the defense and foreign policy community largely came to accept as a truth that it could predictably strengthen deterrence stability by protecting against these "destabilizing" ICBM and BMD systems and preserving mutual vulnerability.

The important point to note in this discussion is that high-confidence deterrence stability came to be defined as the result of secure retaliatory nuclear threats.[63] Although U.S. nuclear strategy

---

60. By the late 1960s U.S. officials believed this "stabilizing" situation had emerged. For example, in 1970 Herbert Scoville, former Deputy Director of the CIA and former Assistant Director of the Arms Control and Disarmament Agency, observed that because each side had established a confident nuclear retaliatory capability, "The U.S. and U.S.S.R. have reached a plateau in the strategic arms race." This view was common and, as it turned out, quite mistaken. See Herbert Scoville and Robert Osborn, *Missile Madness* (Boston: Houghton Mifflin, 1970), 38. See also the discussion in William Foster, "Strategic Weapons: Prospects for Arms Control," *Foreign Affairs* 47, no. 3 (April 1969): 413–21.

61. Apparently Secretary McNamara highly valued this deterrence framework for limitation because it armed him with a logical basis for fending off requests from the military services for additional nuclear capabilities. See, Kaplan, *Wizards of Armageddon*, 318–19.

62. Foster, "Strategic Weapons," 414–15.

63. As McGeorge Bundy observed in 1969, "In light of the certain prospect of retaliation there has been literally no chance at all that any sane political authority, in either the United States or the Soviet Union, would consciously choose to start a nuclear war. This proposition is true for the past, the present and the foreseeable future." Bundy, "To Cap the Volcano," 9.

reportedly never strictly reflected Minimum Deterrence or MAD, Washington officials, acting on this general underlying deterrence framework, believed that they could predictably strengthen deterrence stability by manipulating nuclear threats through both proper U.S. nuclear arms acquisition,[64] and arms control.[65]

War-Fighting uses a different yardstick by which to judge "how much is enough" but ultimately reflects the same Assured Vulnerability paradigm. War-Fighting, although also formulated early in the nuclear era, is associated most closely with the so-called Schlesinger Doctrine of 1974[66] and subsequent War-Fighting

---

64. The United States, for example, decided to limit the number of MX ICBMs on the basis of the Assured Vulnerability paradigm, specifically so that it could not pose a threat to the Soviet retaliatory capability. See, for example, the testimony of Brent Scowcroft in U.S. Senate, Committee on Armed Services, *MX Missile Basing System and Related Issues: Hearings*, 98th Cong., 1st sess. (Washington, D.C.: GPO, 1983), 17–18. Former Secretary McNamara stated that the United States decided to freeze its ICBM force because "we believed in what I am going to call deterrence, in 'assured destruction,' and we felt we could achieve that strategic objective with the number of missiles and warheads we then had." Interview with McNamara in Michael Charlton, *From Deterrence to Defence* (Cambridge: Harvard Univ. Press, 1987), 19.

65. See, for example, Harold Brown, "Strategic Weapons: Security through Limitations," *Foreign Affairs* 47, no. 3 (April 1969): 422–32. There is no doubt that the 1972 ABM Treaty is a reflection of the Assured Vulnerability paradigm. As Paul Doty and Antonia Chayes observe of the treaty: "For the United States, the ABM Treaty was based on three major premises: First, that the only insurance against nuclear war for the foreseeable future remained a stable nuclear deterrent based on invulnerable second-strike forces. Second, that agreed qualitative and quantitative restraints on strategic offensive forces could enhance stability. Third, in the current state of relatively ineffective defenses against nuclear weapons, development and testing of air- or space-based antiballistic missile systems would reduce each side's confidence in its retaliatory capability, erode stability, and undermine incentive to limit strategic offensive forces." "Introduction and Scope of Study," in *Defending Deterrence: Managing the ABM Treaty Regime into the 21st Century*, ed. Antonia Chayes and Paul Doty (Washington, D.C.: Pergamon-Brassey's, 1989), 2–3. This U.S. effort to use arms control to try to limit "destabilizing" weapons, as defined by Assured Vulnerability, has continued through to the present, although progress with the Soviet Union in this regard was not forthcoming. As Brent Scowcroft, John Deutch, and R. James Woolsey stated nearly two decades after the beginning of SALT, "Our major effort over 17 years of arms control negotiations on strategic offensive systems has been dedicated to preserving the survivability of our own silo-based ICBMs. They [the Soviets] have noted our concern about survivability and have cheerfully made it worse with their massive investments in the programs we most want to restrict." "A Small, Survivable, Mobile ICBM," *Washington Post*, 26 December 1986, A23.

66. For a detailed description and assessment of the Schlesinger doctrine and "War-Fighting" developments in U.S. nuclear strategy, see, Keith B. Payne, "The Schlesinger Shift: Return to Rationality," in Keith B. Payne, C. Johnston Conover, and Bruce William Bennett *Nuclear Strategy: Flexibility and Stability* (Santa Monica, Calif: California Seminar on Arms Control and Foreign Policy, 1979), 1–48. For an early discussion of the notion of targeting flexibility, see Morton Kaplan, "Limited Retaliation as a Bargaining Process," in *Limited Strategic War*, ed. Klaus Knorr and Thornton Read (New York: Praeger, 1962), 142–62; and Kaplan, "Problems of Coalition and Deterrence," in *NATO and American Security*, ed. Klaus Knorr (Princeton: Princeton Univ. Press, 1959), 127–50.

developments in U.S. nuclear strategy, such as the Carter Administration's 1980 Presidential Directive (PD)-59.[67]

War-Fighting rejected the notion that threatening population and industry could be an adequate basis for deterrence of highly provocative Soviet behavior. Limiting U.S. nuclear capabilities to a "counter-city" threat, as suggested by Minimum Deterrence and MAD, could undermine the effectiveness of the U.S. deterrence policy by making it appear incredible. The reasoning behind this contention is not complex: U.S. leaders could have significant incentives to withhold retaliation against Soviet cities following a *constrained* Soviet nuclear strike because the Soviet Union could strike first selectively at U.S. nuclear forces and retain a sizable reserve force with which to continue threatening U.S. cities, thereby deterring the U.S. from executing its "counter-city" retaliatory threats. It was argued, therefore, that Soviet leaders could anticipate United States "self-deterrence" under Minimum Deterrence and MAD, and exploit this paralysis of the U.S. deterrence policy.

War-Fighting attempted to address this problem by including as a U.S. requirement the capability to employ strategic nuclear forces selectively against Soviet political and military targets, while continuing to hold in reserve an assured destruction threat. It was argued that whereas Soviet leaders might believe that the United States could be deterred from unleashing "assured destruction" following a limited Soviet attack, a U.S. capability for selective and counter-military strategic strikes would appear to be more usable and therefore a more effective basis for demonstrating the credibility of U.S. strategic threats.[68] Thus War-Fighting established a requirement for strategic forces considered

---

67. For the initial public discussion of PD-59, see Harold Brown, speech at the Naval War College, 20 August 1980, in U.S. Department of Defense, *News Release*, No. 344-80, 20 August 1980; and U.S. Senate, Committee on Foreign Relations, *Nuclear War Strategy: Hearings*, 96th Cong., 2d sess. (Washington, D.C.: GPO, 1981).

68. See for example, statements of James Schlesinger in U.S. Senate, Committee on Foreign Relations, *U.S./U.S.S.R. Strategic Policies*, 93d Cong., 2d sess. (Washington, D.C.: GPO, 1974), 7, 12, 13, and 55; and James Schlesinger, *Annual Defense Department Report, FY 1976 and FY 197T* (Washington, D.C.: GPO, 5 February 1975), I-4. As Glen Snyder observes, this War-Fighting approach, "must stand or fall on its demonstrative or bargaining potency, not on its additional effects . . . . The act of starting reprisals against forces creates a risk for the enemy that we will ultimately attack cities." See Snyder, *Deterrence and Defense*, 200, 211. See also Schelling, "Comment," in *Limited Strategic War*, 256.

"destabilizing" under Minimum Deterrence and MAD; that is, the capability to threaten selectively Soviet military and political targets.[69]

In addition to addressing the possibility for self-deterrence, War-Fighting nuclear force requirements included the capability to threaten hardened military and political targets for deterrence purposes; such targets were said to represent an element of what the Soviet leadership valued. According to Defense Secretary Harold Brown, the U.S. needed a capability to threaten military and political targets for deterrence purposes because "the assets that the Soviet leaders appear to prize . . . are not only their urban industrial facilities but their nuclear and conventional forces and the hardened shelters that protect their political and military control centers, as well as their own lives."[70]

Finally, War-Fighting rejects the view, common to MAD and Minimum Deterrence, that beyond a secure capability to threaten cities, the size of the nuclear arsenal is inconsequential. This tenet of War-Fighting is not a shallow and mechanistic view that the more nuclear firepower a side possesses, the greater will be its deterrent leverage, as some have suggested.[71] Rather, important political influence would be lost internationally, according to this approach to deterrence policy, if the U.S. arsenal were to be judged relatively less capable overall than the opponent's.[72]

---

69. As President Carter said of PD-59, it was intended to target "nuclear launch locations in order to avoid concentrating on population centers, and specifically to destroy the military and industrial capabilities of the Soviet Union." Interview with President Carter in Charlton, *From Deterrence to Defence*, 20.

70. See the testimony of Harold Brown in U.S. Senate, Committee on Armed Services, *MX Missile Basing System and Related Issues: Hearings*, 98th Cong., 1st sess. (Washington, D.C.: GPO, 1983), 7. See the discussion of this shift away from threatening cities per se under the 1974 Schlesinger doctrine in William R. Van Cleave and Roger Barnett, "Strategic Adaptability," *Orbis* 28, no. 3 (fall 1974): 666; and in Donald Rumsfeld, *Annual Defense Department Report FY 1978* (Washington, D.C.: GPO, 17 January 1977): 68.

71. See, for example, the discussion of "War-fighting" by Lebow and Stein, *We All Lost the Cold War*, 348–68.

72. For this reason an important element of the Schlesinger doctrine was the call for "essential equivalence" with the Soviet Union in strategic capability. See James Schlesinger, *Remarks to the Overseas Writer Association*, Overseas Writers Association Luncheon at the International Club, Washington, D.C., 10 January 1974, 11, 13 (mimeographed); James Schlesinger, *Annual Defense Department Report, FY 1976 and FY 197T*, II–8; and James Schlesinger, *U.S./U.S.S.R. Strategic Policies*, 41, 56. Harold Brown concurred with this need to maintain a balance of capabilities vis-à-vis the Soviet Union. See Harold Brown, *Thinking about National Security* (Boulder, Colo.: Westview, 1983), 53–55.

In sum, the War-Fighting approach to deterrence policy includes nuclear force requirements well beyond those of Minimum Deterrence and MAD. These requirements include capabilities deemed "destabilizing" and "overkill" by the other policy approaches. These War-Fighting differences led some commentators to conclude wrongly that this approach did not fit within the overarching Assured Vulnerability deterrence framework.[73] However, War-Fighting—reflected in the declared policy of the United States from 1974 until the demise of the Soviet Union—is well within this general approach to deterrence. Although it differs from Minimum Deterrence and MAD in defining an adequate deterrent threat, it shares their basic precepts that the opponent will behave rationally and sensibly, that deterrence stability can confidently be based on the proper retaliatory nuclear threats, and that the stability of deterrence can be manipulated predictably by adjusting the character of the U.S. retaliatory threat. As Colin Gray observed in 1984 with regard to the War-Fighting initiatives of U.S. policy: "U.S. strategic policy still, at root, relies on a punishment strategy. Indeed, U.S. [War-Fighting] nuclear strategy is a sophisticated variant of the 'competition in risk-taking' described so eloquently by Thomas Schelling more than twenty years ago. Today, preeminently, the United States plans to punish the Soviet state and its executive instruments rather than its captive, or acquiescent, society. The official U.S. concept of deterrence depends on the idea that a Soviet leadership, anticipating severe damage to its most cherished values, will be deterred from choosing to fight."[74]

---

73. See, for example, Robert Scheer, *With Enough Shovels: Reagan, Bush and Nuclear War* (New York: Random House, 1982).

74. Gray, *Nuclear Strategy and Strategic Planning*, 41. Harold Brown gave official credence to this point that War-Fighting did not move beyond the Assured Vulnerability framework. "In the interests of stability we avoid the capability of eliminating the other side's deterrent, insofar as we might be able to do so. In short, we must be quite willing—as we have been for some time—to accept the principle of mutual deterrence, and design our defense posture in light of that principle." Harold Brown, *Department of Defense Annual Report Fiscal Year 1980* (Washington, D.C.: GPO, 25 January 1979), 61. President Carter made much the same point in explaining that Presidential Directive-59 (PD-59) did not reflect a rejection of mutual deterrence through mutual vulnerability. See Charlton, *From Deterrence to Defence*, 20. It should be noted that PD-41 of September 1978 directed the U.S. civil defense program to enhance the survivability of the American people and its leadership in the event of nuclear war. Although this directive does show interest in providing "some increase in the number of surviving population and for greater continuity of government should deterrence and escalation control fail," it also states that its purpose

Although some proponents of War-Fighting find it offensive to be placed in the same camp as Minimum Deterrence and MAD, their favored approach does not differ from the latter in its fundamental assumptions: to deter is a matter of establishing the necessary strategic threat vis-à-vis a rational, sensible opponent, and adjusting that balance is the key to achieving a predictably stable deterrence relationship. Indeed, how does War-Fighting propose to rectify the inadequacies of Minimum Deterrence and MAD? By adding layers to and redefining requirements for the U.S. retaliatory nuclear threat to make it more credible and provide "intra-war" deterrence vis-à-vis a sensible foe.[75] In short, War-Fighting seeks to repair the flaws it sees in Minimum Deterrence and MAD essentially by adjusting and further manipulating the nuclear threat for deterrence purposes. As Fred Iklé observes, "Faith in nonuse [of nuclear weapons] made it easy for both hawks and doves to place their confidence in deterrence."[76]

Assured Vulnerability and Unwarranted Confidence

The Assured Vulnerability paradigm assumes the character of the opponent and the context to be amenable to deterrence policies, and therefore it largely sets aside important contextual factors to focus on the character of the strategic balance as the determinant

---

is to "enhance deterrence and stability" and specifically "does not suggest any change in continuing U.S. reliance on strategic offensive forces as the preponderant factor in maintaining deterrence." See Jimmy Carter, Presidential Directive-41, to Vice President, Secretary of State, Secretary of Defense, Subject: U.S. Civil Defense Policy, September 29, 1978, SECRET (Declassified 23 June 1980).

75. War-Fighting as policy never passed the central test for transcending Assured Vulnerability because, as Colin Gray rightly observes, it prescribed "no physical shield for the United States." See Gray, *Nuclear Strategy and Strategic Planning*, 41. The Strategic Defense Initiative (SDI) was introduced by President Reagan in 1983 as a long-term means to use defensive technology to provide a shield and exit the mutual–vulnerability–based deterrence relationship with the Soviet Union. This was, in fact, a conscious challenge to the Assured Vulnerability deterrence framework. Following a brief period in the mid-1980s, however, the SDI came to be presented by Reagan and Bush administration officials almost entirely as a means of enhancing deterrence by protecting U.S. retaliatory forces. This transition of the SDI, of course, fit perfectly with the Assured Vulnerability paradigm. For a detailed discussion of this transition in the rationale for the SDI from a challenge to Assured Vulnerability to a reflection of it, see Keith B. Payne, *Missile Defense in the 21st Century: Protection against Limited Threats* (Boulder, Colo.: Westview, 1991), 6–12.

76. Iklé, "The Second Coming of the Nuclear Age," 123.

of stability:[77] to establish a reliable and predictable deterrence policy simply involves acquiring the proper retaliatory nuclear threats. The immediate cause of instability would be the undermining of these threats. Because nuclear threats could be controlled and adjusted by changing the force structure, it was considered relatively easy to identify how to adjust the forces as necessary to ensure deterrence stability. Consequently, the effectiveness of U.S. deterrence policy could be maintained with confidence.

This brief review of Minimum Deterrence, MAD, and War-Fighting demonstrates the broad consensus on Assured Vulnerability precepts common to these various approaches to strategic deterrence policy. All accept the assumption of a sensible, rational opponent and that threats of nuclear retaliation are a reliable basis for shaping that opponent's behavior. All accept that adjustments to the strategic nuclear arsenals can have predictable effects on deterrence stability.[78] The major variation among these three is with regard to their specific definitions of the required retaliatory nuclear threat and the force structure thought necessary to support that threat.

These three policy approaches, each essentially accepting the basic assumptions of Assured Vulnerability concerning the character of the opponent and how to deter, covered virtually the entire spectrum of debate. Despite the obvious differences in defining "how much is enough," they illustrate an overwhelming and bipartisan consensus on a particular deterrence framework. This consensus often was overshadowed by the vehemence of the debate over what essentially were the details, albeit the important

---

77. For example, in Herbert Scoville's basic presentation of "strategic stability," he identifies "four key factors" as determinants of stability; they exclusively involve strategic capabilities. As he observes, in the bipolar U.S.-Soviet relationship, "Strategic decisions can still be based primarily on analyses of the forces of these two countries alone." See Scoville and Osborne, *Missile Madness*, 25–27. Herbert York, a well known senior U.S. official and academic commentator on deterrence "stability" during the Cold War, similarly discussed only the technical characteristics of strategic forces as those factors that "threaten to upset the strategic stability." See his classic treatment of the issue in *Race to Oblivion* (New York: Simon and Schuster, 1971), 173–87.

78. As Lebow and Stein rightly observe following their assessment of U.S. nuclear deterrence policies and "real-world" crises, the various U.S. policy approaches "all mistakenly equate stability with specific arms configurations." *We All Lost the Cold War*, 366.

details, of how many and what types of weapons constituted an adequate retaliatory nuclear threat. In short, with the overwhelming acceptance of Assured Vulnerability precepts, a consensus emerged that strategic deterrence could be understood and manipulated predictably by adjusting the nuclear threat and arsenal. This conclusion is obvious over the wide spectrum of U.S. thought on strategic deterrence policy.

The Assured Vulnerability paradigm remains the theoretical basis for those who now claim confidently, without knowledge of the specific opponent or context, that because nuclear deterrence worked during the Cold War it will work in the future. Based on the Assured Vulnerability assumption of a generically sensible opponent, ensuring deterrence still is considered a matter of threat—so long as the United States has a nuclear retaliatory capability, "they won't dare" to provoke us in the extreme. Deterrence will work because we have the capability, as various commentators have so gingerly put it, to squash the opponent "like a bug," turn the opponent "into a sea of radioactive glass" or "a hole in the ocean," or to "erase them from the map." Clearly, the consensus and confidence about ensuring deterrence at the past U.S.-Soviet strategic level has been transferred, without any apparent review or adjustment, to expectations about how to ensure that deterrence will work more broadly in the second nuclear age.

This view, that deterrence essentially can be made certain through the proper nuclear threat, is reflected in the most recent presentation of U.S. national security strategy: "The United States will retain a triad of strategic nuclear forces sufficient to deter any future hostile foreign leadership from acting against our vital interest."

To do this, what is required? We must "maintain nuclear forces of sufficient size and capability to hold at risk a broad range of assets valued by [the opponent's] political and military leaders."[79] There is no suggestion of doubt that we can deter with confidence by manipulating the nuclear threat. The Assured Vulnerability paradigm is alive and well.

---

79. Quote from William J. Clinton, *A National Strategy of Engagement and Enlargement* (Washington, D.C.: White House, February 1995), 15.

During the Cold War this deterrence focus on the strategic balance may have made some sense; other important factors such as the credibility of our commitment came to be largely assumed. In U.S.-Soviet strategic deterrence relations, U.S. retaliatory threats were posed to deter attacks on "intrinsic interests," that is, national survival or interests well established by history and a manifest military commitment as "vital" (such as the security of Western Europe). Such deterrence commitments are considered highly credible given the manifest national priority placed on the interests they are intended to preserve. Because the credibility of the threat was assumed, as was the sensible character of the opponent, the key factor determining deterrence effectiveness was reduced to the strategic balance—the nuclear capabilities behind deterrence threats.

Yet this approach will be inappropriate in at least some future cases because in the second nuclear age factors other than the character of the nuclear threat will shape the success or failure of U.S. deterrence policies. For example, the credibility of a U.S. deterrence commitment for an "intrinsic interest" is less likely to be questioned by an informed and sensible opponent than the credibility of a commitment on behalf of lesser regional interests.[80] Empirical analyses suggest that an informed and sensible opponent simply is unlikely to attach the same level of credibility to deterrence commitments made on behalf of interests that are not manifestly "intrinsic."[81] A primary issue, then, for deterrence operating predictably is whether there is a mutual understanding of the character of the interests involved. Are both sides protecting

---

80. See the discussion in Robert Jervis, "Deterrence Theory Reconsidered," *World Politics* 31, no. 2 (January 1979): 289–324; and Watman and Wilkening, *U.S. Regional Deterrence Strategies*, 6–7. As Thomas Schelling observed in this regard, "The difference between the national homeland and everything 'abroad' is the difference between threats *that are inherently credible*, even if unspoken, and threats that have to be made credible." (my emphasis). See Schelling, *Arms and Influence*, 36.

81. See the discussion in Elli Lieberman, *Deterrence Theory: Success or Failure in Arab-Israeli Wars?* (Washington, D.C.: National Defense University, Institute for National Strategic Studies, October 1995), 64. As Alexander George and Richard Smoke observe in their ground-breaking inductive analysis of deterrence, "What tends to be overlooked in traditional commitment theory is that effective deterrence and effective signaling require in the first instance that the interests of the United States be sufficiently engaged by what is at stake in the area or country in question. Commitments which rest on relatively weak national motivation are more likely to be challenged." *Deterrence in American Foreign Policy: Theory and Practice* (New York: Columbia Univ. Press, 1974), 560.

intrinsic interests and, if so, do both recognize the context as such? If the U.S. interest does not benefit from a historical legacy demonstrating that it is intrinsic, is it at all possible for the United States to establish the necessary credibility for its deterrence commitment? Deterrence in these cases will be much more than simply a matter of wielding a threat of a particular size, because the credibility of the threat cannot simply be taken for granted. This is an important distinction; as historic analyses demonstrate, establishing credible deterrence commitments may be very difficult.[82] It is far from certain that we will be able to do so reliably vis-à-vis opponents in the second nuclear age.

In addition, as discussed above, a problem with the deterrence paradigm in general is that it posits a sensible, rational, and informed opponent. Perhaps, in U.S.-Soviet relations such an assumption was accurate enough.[83] Although the proposition is debatable, we may have been sufficiently familiar with the Soviet Union to anticipate the leaders' perceptions and how they defined reasonable, sensible behavior; therefore, we may have been able to predict within an acceptable margin of error how they would react to deterrence threats under various conditions. Consequently, it

---

82. The primary conclusion of a recent analysis of deterrence based on historical case studies is that to establish credibility for commitments covering extrinsic interests is very difficult and may well include a demonstrative willingness to go to war. "Thus the dilemma for leaders is that acting tough may require going to war, which is costly immediately and only may have payoffs in the future. . . . Unfortunately, in order to make deterrence work in the conventional world states may have to fight wars to create reputations for capability and will." Lieberman, *Deterrence Theory*, 64–65. See also Watman and Wilkening, *U.S. Regional Deterrence Strategies*, 62–64.

83. Even in U.S.-Soviet relations it must be noted that the mutual understanding necessary for predictable behavior may have been lacking on occasion. As former Secretary of Defense McNamara noted with regard to the Cuban missile crisis, following discussions with Soviet and Cuban participants in the crisis, "how close the planet came to nuclear disaster. . . . It was a dramatic demonstration of fallibility—of the degree to which all parties were captives of misinformation, misjudgement and miscalculation." See Robert McNamara, "Nobody Needs Nukes," *New York Times*, 23 February 1993, 21. And, as late as 1983, the Soviet Union appears to have been sufficiently confused about U.S. decision-making, intentions, and behavior to have misinterpreted some U.S. actions as active preparation for nuclear war, and to have engaged in initial responsive preparations. Oleg Gordievski, a former senior Soviet intelligence officer, has reported that in 1983 Warsaw Pact intelligence was convinced that NATO was preparing to launch a massive surprise attack. See Gordon Brook-Shepard, *The Storm Birds* (New York: Weidenfeld and Nicolson, 1989), 329–35. See also the discussion of this incident in Bruce Blair, *The Logic of Accidental Nuclear War* (Washington, D.C.: Brookings Institution, 1993), 180–81; and "Operation RYAN," in *Comrade Kryuchkov's Instructions: Top Secret Files on KGB Foreign Operations, 1975–1985*, ed. Christopher Andrew and Oleg Gordievsky (Stanford: Stanford University Press, 1993), 67–90.

may have been reasonable in deterrence relations with the Soviet Union to assume that the credibility of U.S. threats and the character of the Soviet leadership facilitated the efficacy of deterrence, thus allowing us to focus on adjusting the strategic balance as the determinant of stability.

Yet we know that rational opponents do not always behave in accordance with our own definition of "sensible," and we frequently have not accurately anticipated challengers' behavior. Absent an adequate appreciation of the specific opponent's values, goals, determination, perceptions, risk propensities, and so forth, and absent the capacity to make the U.S. threat credible in the eyes of the opponent based on that knowledge, predictions of that challenger's likely response to U.S. threats under varying conditions will involve a considerable amount of speculation and guesswork. In the context of the variety of possible opponents in the second nuclear age, some of which may be quite unfamiliar to us,[84] assuming that positive contextual factors will be favorable for deterrence is likely to lead to surprises. Such an assumption hardly can serve as the basis for confident assertions about the future workings of deterrence. As Alexander George, a pioneer in the analysis of deterrence theory and policy, notes: "A critical problem with this strategy [deterrence] is that it rests on the assumption of pure rationality on the part of the opponent, and on his ability to recognize and act upon his self-interest. Of course, this assumption is inadequate—you must know the other side

---

84. Considerable ignorance of potential challengers in the second nuclear age has been acknowledged by officials in the intelligence community. For example, Director of Central Intelligence John Deutch recently acknowledged that the intelligence community knows "very little about Beijing's future leadership and intentions" and is similarly ignorant regarding North Korea. Quoted in Tim Weiner, "CIA Chief Defends Secrecy, in Spending and Spying, to Senate," *New York Times*, 23 February 1996, A5. The Director of the Defense Intelligence Agency, Lt. Gen. James Clapper, similarly observed that "the Intelligence Community is unable to decipher North Korea's political intentions because of a paucity of reliable human sources and a lack of insight into the political decisionmaking process in North Korea." In U.S. Senate, Select Committee on Intelligence, *Current and Projected National Security Threats to the United States and Its Interests Abroad*, 103d Congress, 2d sess. (Washington, D.C.: GPO, 1994), 95. And, as U.S. Ambassador April Glaspie said of the genesis of the Gulf war, "We didn't understand Saddam Hussein." Quoted in Don Oberdorfer, "Glaspie Says Saddam Guilty of Deception," *Washington Post*, 21 March 1991, A-23.

well enough to understand, in the particular case, the political, psychological, and cultural aspects of rationality."[85]

In short, the Assured Vulnerability paradigm encourages unwarranted confidence when applied to the regional deterrence considerations of the second nuclear age. Because the United States will confront challengers with which it is relatively unfamiliar and whose intentions, will, and commitment are not well understood, it seems likely that the prospects for unpredictable behavior will grow—again, hardly the basis for definitive statements about deterrence.

With deductive logic, intuition, hope, and selected historical illustrations at its foundation, the Assured Vulnerability deterrence framework served as the basis for confident U.S. Cold War deterrence policies and now constitutes the basis for belief that deterrence will be similarly reliable in the second nuclear age. In 1994, as the nominee for the position of commander in chief, U.S. Strategic Command, Vice Admiral H.G. Chiles was asked by Senator Sam Nunn about the role of nuclear weapons for deterrence in the new strategic environment. Admiral Chiles's response reflected this extension of basic Cold War assumptions about deterrence into the second nuclear age.

> Our deterrence strategy is founded on the theory that an adversarial state or coalition group will act according to the logic of national or group self-interest. While they may view their self-interests through a different cultural perspective, as a minimum they must seriously consider the full range of possible repercussions prior to attacking the United States or our allies with any weapon of mass destruction. Therefore, I believe our nuclear weapons can and do serve as a deterrent to conventional aggression against the United States and our allies.[86]

Of course, a challenger may "seriously consider the full range of possible repercussions." But to claim that "as a minimum they

---

85.   Quoted in "Speaking with Alexander George about 'Coercive Diplomacy,'" *United States Institute of Peace Journal* 4, no. 5 (October 1991): 2.

86.   Statement in U.S. Senate, Committee on Armed Services, *Nominations before the Senate Armed Services Committee*, 103d Cong., 2d sess. (Washington, D.C.: GPO, 1994), 227.

must" do so, as Admiral Chiles states, clearly is an expression of hope, not fact, and hardly the basis for such confidence about deterrence. How could Assured Vulnerability, with its particular assumptions about how challengers will make decisions, achieve such acceptance, indeed establishing a virtual lock on strategic thinking in the United States? The answers are speculative. It is possible, however, to observe that Assured Vulnerability is elegant and simple. It reduces deterrence "instability" to the single cause of the force structure, and then offers a solution to the problem that governments can effect; that is, adjust the force structure as necessary. It is reassuring because it confirms what we would like to believe: The behavior of our opponents will be predictable and can be controlled by our actions. It tells us that it is within our power to control our future. What could be more comforting? It tells us what we want to believe.

In Donald Kagan's tour de force *On the Origins of War*, he contends that it is a "special characteristic" of Western civilization to believe that we have the power to control the physical and social environment to improve society, even to produce peace. "So," according to Kagan, "it is not surprising to come upon these hopeful expectations by men of the Enlightenment and their intellectual heirs." Since the eighteenth century the Western enlightened mind has viewed war as abnormal, irrational, unprofitable, and stemming from a wayward drive for national gain. Because modern Western civilization, in contrast to Greek and Roman, prefers to minimize military preparation and expenditure, the preferred solution to military threats is to enlighten opposing leaders to the truth about the irrationality of war, for they will then choose peace.[87]

Assured Vulnerability is a perfect expression of this "special characteristic" of Western civilization, its view of war, and the preferred mechanism for preventing war: War is irrational; when made aware of this, leaders will choose peace. Our primary burden in orchestrating this happy situation is the *relatively* inexpensive and easy task of maintaining an adequate nuclear

---

87. Donald Kagan, *On the Origins of War* (New York: Doubleday, 1995), 3–4, 569–72.

retaliatory threat (variously defined).[88] Perhaps it is, in fact, little wonder that Assured Vulnerability has achieved such prominence. It is an expression of centuries of enlightened Western thinking and hope about war and its prevention. Attractive as this deterrence paradigm is, the question to which we must return is whether it can serve as a useful basis for U.S. deterrence policy in the second nuclear age.

---

88.   Alexander George makes this point vis-à-vis coercive diplomacy in general: "It must be recognized that coercive diplomacy is a beguiling strategy insofar as it offers an attractive possibility for achieving one's objective without having to rely on force." *Forceful Persuasion*, xv.

Chapter 4
Success, Motivation, Mistakes, and Uncertainty

The reasons for seeking more power are often not merely the search for security or material advantage. Among them are demands for greater prestige, respect, and deference, in short, honor.

—Donald Kagan, *On the Origins of War*

Senior U.S. officials and prominent commentators, reflecting Cold War–era confidence and assumptions, now express certainty concerning the prospective effectiveness of deterrence in the second nuclear age—even to the point of identifying specifically those countries against which deterrence will surely work. Chapters 2 and 3, however, suggest several reasons why the Cold War strategic deterrence paradigm may be inappropriate as the basis for confidence for the second nuclear age: (1) whereas the duties of U.S. Cold War deterrence policies were to prevent Soviet nuclear or conventional attack, in the second nuclear age, as the proliferation of WMD and delivery systems continues apace, U.S. deterrence policies will need to be adequate for the possibly more stressing mission of "deterring the deterrent" of a desperate challenger; (2) whereas during the Cold War the credibility of the U.S. commitment was assumed, given the intrinsic U.S. interests at stake, the regional disputes of the second nuclear age will likely involve intrinsic interests for the challenger and nonintrinsic interests for the United States, with corresponding perceptions of reduced credibility for U.S. commitments; (3) whereas, based on decades of close interaction with Soviet leaders, the U.S. may have understood that Cold War opponent sufficiently well to preclude gross surprises, in the second nuclear age such familiarity will likely be lacking in some, perhaps many cases. A mutual lack of familiarity is apparent, for example, in U.S. relations with China, North Korea, Iraq, and Iran.

In short, the context for deterrence policies will be sufficiently different from the past that we must reconsider how to apply deterrence theory, and how much confidence reasonably can be placed in deterrence policies. The question is not whether deterrence policies can or cannot work in the second nuclear age; that they can under the proper conditions is clear. Rather, the question is whether deterrence policies can be made to work with the degree of predictability and reliability claimed by U.S. officials, or at least with a predictability that provides U.S. officials with a reasonable level of confidence.

There are numerous factors that can undermine the predictable functioning of deterrence policies. Some of these factors have long been recognized, such as the possibility of unexpected behavior as is discussed in Chapter 3. Nevertheless, the Cold War's Assured Vulnerability paradigm focused nearly exclusively on adjusting the character of nuclear threats as the means of "ensuring" deterrence success—as if it could be assumed that the proper nuclear threat would guarantee deterrence. The notion that the proper nuclear threat can make deterrence "conclusive," despite the potential for human error, is readily apparent in the following statement by former Secretary of Defense Harold Brown: "It should be noted that political leaders in the past—aggressive, but not necessarily irrational—have often made wishful, mistaken, and foolish estimates of consequences that have led to catastrophic wars. Nuclear deterrence must therefore be conclusive. It must present such a certainty of destructive retaliation that no chain of reasoning would allow a decision maker contemplating the initiation of a strategic war to conclude that such an attack would be anything other than the worst possible choice."[1]

Brown properly identifies as important factors in the success of deterrence policies both the U.S. threat and the challenger's perception of U.S. will: "a certainty of destructive retaliation" is necessary to make deterrence "conclusive." The question, however, is whether the objective identified by Brown is at all possible: Can we, by our policies, make deterrence "conclusive?" Is it in our power to ensure that a challenger always sees an attack on the

---

1. Harold Brown, *Thinking about National Security* (Boulder, Colo.: Westview, 1983), 50–51.

United States as "the worst possible choice," as frequently is claimed by officials and commentators, for the second nuclear age?

To be sure, in some cases there is evidence that nuclear weapons have had the hoped-for effect of limiting the escalation of a crisis.[2] Presented below is a recent case in which U.S. nuclear weapons and ad hoc deterrence policies appear to have been successful and to reflect what Sun Tzu calls "the acme of skill."

Success and Failure in the Gulf War

A puzzling question following the 1991 Gulf war involved deterrence. Why did Saddam Hussein *not* use the chemical and biological weapons at his disposal in the infamous Iraqi missile strikes against Israel and Saudi Arabia? Reports by Ambassador Rolf Ekeus of the United Nations Special Commission for the Disarmament of Iraq (UNSCOM) indicate that in addition to the production of highly lethal nerve agents, Saddam Hussein had prepared for use 25 missile warheads and 166 bombs filled with deadly biological agents such as botulinum toxin, anthrax, and aflatoxin.[3] Why did Saddam Hussein not use these weapons of mass destruction?

Although Iraqi air power was shut down almost immediately in the war, Iraq launched 88 conventionally armed Scud missiles against targets in Israel and Saudi Arabia. These missile strikes continued until the end of the war. In one attack, pieces of an Iraqi

---

2. For example, as was noted in Chapter 2, it appears that the decision-making of the U.S. leadership in the Cuban missile crisis was shaped by the recognition of a nuclear threat. Richard Ned Lebow and Janice Gross Stein have concluded, following their assessment of the crisis, that a general appreciation of mutual nuclear deterrence, "had a restraining effect on both Kennedy and Khrushchev." *We All Lost the Cold War* (Princeton: Princeton Univ. Press, 1995), 356.

3. See Barbara Crossette, "Crash Nuclear Program by Iraq Disclosed," *New York Times*, 26 August 1995, 3; Stewart Stogel and Ben Barber, "Iraq Entered Gulf War with Viral Weapons Ready," *Washington Times*, 11 September 1995, 13; R. Jeffrey Smith, "U.N. Says Iraqis Prepared Germ Weapons in Gulf War," *Washington Post*, 26 August 1995, A1, A19; summary of remarks by Ambassador Rolf Ekeus, "Unearthing Iraq's Weapons of Mass Destruction: A Progress Report," *Policywatch*, no. 175, 20 November 1995, 1–2; and United Nations, Security Council, *Report of the Secretary-General on the Status of the Implementation of the Special Commission's Plan for the Ongoing Monitoring and Verification of Iraq's Compliance with Relevant Parts of Section C of Security Council Resolution 687 (1991)*, S/1995/864, 11 October 1995.

missile that broke up in flight struck a makeshift U.S. barracks in Dhahran, Saudi Arabia, killing 28 and wounding 100. This single strike accounted for the largest number of U.S. combat casualties in the war. In Israel and the United States there was concern that Iraq would use chemical weapons.[4] The anticipation of such attacks led Israeli citizens to take shelter in specially sealed rooms and to wear gas masks. Although Iraq did not use chemical warheads, Scud strikes directly inflicted more than 250 Israeli casualties and were indirectly responsible for a dozen deaths, including children, resulting from the improper use of gas masks.[5] U.N. officials have stated that Iraqi bombs and missiles armed with WMD contained enough biological agents to kill hundreds of thousands.[6] U.S. officials have confirmed that if Iraq had used anthrax, for example, the military and civilian casualty levels could have been enormous.[7]

Saddam Hussein appears to be neither a philanthropist nor particularly humane. Why then did he *not* use the available chemical or biological weapons? Was he deterred by the prospect of nuclear retaliation? Israeli analysts frequently suggest that the Israeli nuclear threat deterred Iraqi chemical use. In this regard, it should be noted that during a CNN interview on 2 February 1991, U.S. Defense Secretary Dick Cheney was asked about the potential for Israeli nuclear retaliation to Iraqi chemical strikes. Secretary Cheney observed that this would be a decision that "the Israelis

---

4. President Bush has stated that, "One of my big worries as commander-in-chief, which was shared by our military, was the fact that he might use chemical weapons. . . . We lived in fear of it." President Bush in *A Gulf War Exclusive: President Bush Talking with David Frost*, Transcript no. 51, 16 January 1996, 5. General Norman Schwarzkopf, commander in chief of coalition forces, and General Walt Boomer, commander of U.S. Marines, also anticipated Iraqi chemical use. See their statements in, *Frontline*, no. 1408, *The Gulf War*, *Part II*, 10 January 1996, transcript, 3–4. See also Youssef M. Ibrahim, "Israel Expecting Missiles from Iraq in Case of a War," *New York Times*, 1 January 1991, 1.

5. See the discussion in Moshe Arens, *Broken Covenant* (New York: Simon and Schuster, 1995), 201. See also Senator Arlen Specter, "Statistics on Missile Scud Attacks on Israel," *Congressional Record-Senate*, 5 March 1991, S2689.

6. R. Jeffrey Smith, "U.N. says Iraqis Prepared Germ Weapons," A1. For a comparison of the lethality of conventional, chemical, biological, and nuclear weapons see Steve Fetter, "Ballistic Missiles and Weapons of Mass Destruction: What Is the Threat? What Should Be Done?" *International Security* 16, no. 1 (summer 1992): 27.

7. Presentation by Dr. William Shuler, deputy for counterproliferation, Office of the Assistant to the Secretary of Defense for Atomic Energy, 13 December 1995, Seventh Annual SO/LIC Symposium, Washington Sheraton, Washington, D.C.

would have to make—but I would think that [Hussein] has to be cautious in terms of how he proceeds in his attacks against Israel." The following day, when asked about Secretary Cheney's statement, Israeli Defense Minister Moshe Arens replied, "I think he said that Saddam has reasons to worry—yes, he does have reasons to worry."[8] This reply, and Secretary Cheney's original statement, in which he did not object to the premise of the question or express disapproval of the possibility of Israeli nuclear retaliation, at least to Israeli analysts, was a key to deterring Iraqi chemical weapons use.[9]

The possible direct U.S. role in nuclear deterrence in this case also should be highlighted. On 9 January 1991, Secretary of State James Baker expressed a relatively clear and severe deterrent threat to Iraqi Foreign Minister Tariq Aziz in Geneva: "Before we cross to the other side—that is, if the conflict starts, God forbid, and chemical or biological weapons are used against our forces— the American people would demand revenge, and we have the means to implement this."[10]

President Bush also sent a strongly worded message to Saddam Hussein in the form of a letter delivered to Tariq Aziz by Secretary Baker: "Let me state, too, that the United States will not tolerate the use of chemical or biological weapons or the destruction of Kuwait's oil fields and installations. . . . The American people would demand the strongest possible response. You and your country will pay a terrible price if you order unconscionable acts of this sort."[11]

Secretary of Defense Cheney linked U.S. nuclear threats even more explicitly to Iraqi use of WMD: "The other point that needs to be made, and it's one I have made previously, is that he

8. Akiva Eldar, "'Saddam Would Have Reason to Worry,' Says Arens When Asked about Unconventional Weapons," *Ha' aretz*, 4 February 1991, 1.

9. As discussed by Shai Feldman of Tel Aviv University's Jaffee Center for Strategic Studies and Amatzia Baram of Haifa University in their respective papers presented at the conference on Regional Stability in the Middle East: Arab and Israeli Concepts of Deterrence and Defense, hosted by the United States Institute of Peace, 17–19 June 1991, Washington, D.C.

10. *Baghdad INA*, 9 January 1991, translated and presented in "INA reports Minutes of Aziz-Baker Meeting," FBIS-NES-92-009, 14 January 1992, 27.

11. Reprinted in *U.S. Department of State Dispatch, Persian Gulf*, 2, no. 2, 14 January 1991, 25.

[Hussein] needs to be made aware that the President will have available the full spectrum of capabilities. And were Saddam Hussein foolish enough to use weapons of mass destruction, the U.S. response would be absolutely overwhelming and it would be devastating. He has to take that into consideration, it seems to me, before he embarks upon a course of using those kinds of capabilities."[12]

These statements by then-ranking U.S. and Israeli officials, while not explicitly threatening nuclear retaliation, certainly imply the possibility for it. Nuclear threats would appear to be a possible explanation for Iraqi restraint with regard to chemical and biological weapons. Until confirmed by credible Iraqi sources, however, such a conclusion could remain no more than informed speculation. Recently, however, apparently authoritative accounts of Iraqi wartime decision-making on this issue have emerged. In August 1995, Iraqi Foreign Minister Tariq Aziz reported to Ambassador Ekeus that Iraq was deterred from using its WMD because the Iraqi leadership had interpreted Washington's threats of grievous retaliation as meaning *nuclear* retaliation.[13]

Tariq Aziz's explanation has been corroborated by a senior Iraqi defector, General Wafic Al Sammarai, former head of Iraqi military intelligence. General Sammarai stated, "Some of the Scud missiles were loaded with chemical warheads, but they were not used. They were kept hidden throughout the war. We didn't use them because the other side had a deterrent force."[14] General Sammarai added, "I do not think Saddam was capable of taking a decision to use chemical weapons or biological weapons, or any other type of weapons against the allied troops, because the warning was quite severe, and quite effective. The allied troops were certain to use nuclear arms and the price will be too dear and too high."[15]

12. Public Statements of Richard B. Cheney, Secretary of Defense, 4 (Washington, D.C.: Historical Office, Office of the Secretary of Defense, 1990): 2547.

13. Presented in R. Jeffrey Smith, "U.N. Says Iraqis Prepared Germ Weapons," A19.

14. *The Gulf War, Part I*, statement by General Wafic Al Sammarai, *Frontline*, no. 1407, 9 January 1996, transcript, 12.

15. See the statements by General Wafic Al Sammarai, in *Frontline*, "The Gulf War, Parts I and II," 9 and 10 January 1996. Comprehensive background interviews available via Internet Website www.wgbh.org.

In 1995 Brent Scowcroft, President Bush's national security advisor during the Gulf war, revealed publicly that the U.S. leaders had in fact decided that the United States would *not* respond to Iraqi WMD use with nuclear weapons. Rather, according to Scowcroft, the U.S. would have expanded its conventional attacks against Iraqi targets.[16] And President Bush has stated that "it [nuclear use] was not something that we really contemplated at all."[17] Nevertheless, according to the accounts by Tariq Aziz and General Sammarai, the Iraqi leadership believed that the U.S. would have retaliated with nuclear weapons, and that expectation deterred, as clearly was intended by U.S. officials.

This explanation by senior Iraqi officials suggests the error of those who have asserted with certainty that nuclear weapons were "incredible as a deterrent and therefore irrelevant" in the Gulf war.[18] Those who have attempted to use the Gulf war to demonstrate that nuclear weapons will be relatively less important for deterrence in the second nuclear age than they were during the Cold War need to reconsider their case.

Of course, the accounts by Tariq Aziz and General Sammarai of the rationale for Iraqi restraint do not close the issue; they do, however, suggest that U.S. and possibly Israeli nuclear deterrence were at least part of the answer as to why Saddam Hussein did not use WMD.

This case also illustrates the difficulties involved in demonstrating how and why deterrence worked on one specific occasion but not another. For example, if U.S. nuclear weapons deterred Saddam from using chemical and biological weapons, why did the United States not deter the invasion of Kuwait in the first place? Surely Saddam knew of U.S. nuclear might at the time of the invasion. Then U.S. ambassador to Iraq, April Glaspie, claimed following the war that she had expressed clear U.S. warnings to

---

16. See the transcript of the statements by Brent Scowcroft, NBC News *Meet the Press*, 27 August 1995, 10.

17. *Gulf War Exclusive*, 5. Then-Secretary of State James Baker also states that President Bush "had also decided that U.S. forces would not retaliate with chemical or nuclear weapons if the Iraqis attacked with chemical munitions." James Baker, *The Politics of Diplomacy* (New York: Putnam, 1995), 359.

18. Carl Kaysen, Robert McNamara, and George Rathjens, "Nuclear Weapons after the Cold War," *Foreign Affairs* 70, no. 4 (fall 1991): 102.

Saddam concerning Kuwait. The United States, she emphasized to him, "would not countenance violence or in fact threat of intimidation" toward Kuwait.[19] Yet, following what Ambassador Glaspie described as "clear and repeated" U.S. warnings, Iraq invaded Kuwait. Either U.S. deterrence policy failed in this case, or the United States failed to apply a deterrence policy. If it failed, we have an interesting example of deterrence failing to prevent the invasion but effectively preventing the Iraqi use of WMD during the ensuing conflict.

Sir Michael Howard describes the Iraqi invasion as "a classic example of the failure of deterrence making necessary the exercise of compellance," that is, militarily removing Iraqi forces from Kuwait.[20] According to Ambassador Glaspie, deterrence did not work initially because the United States misunderstood the Iraqi leader. "We foolishly did not realize he was stupid, that he did not believe our clear and repeated warning that we would support our vital interests."[21]

Is Saddam Hussein "stupid," as Ambassador Glaspie claimed in language unusual for a diplomat? Were Ambassador Glaspie's warnings anything but clear and repeated? Did Saddam not appreciate that he was being warned? Or did he hear those initial warnings but not take them seriously enough—judging the prospective gains of invasion to outweigh the likely costs? Analyses of the Gulf war have suggested that U.S. expressions of concern regarding the security of Kuwait—"clear and repeated" as they may have been—were not highly regarded by Saddam. U.S. threats appear to have lacked credibility because Saddam considered the United States "an effete and indolent society no longer willing to risk significant casualties on foreign battlefields," a society that would not actually go to war to overturn Iraq's conquest of Kuwait.[22]

---

19. Quoted in Don Oberdorfer, "Glaspie Says Saddam Is Guilty of Deception," *Washington Post*, 21 March 1991, A23.

20. Sir Michael Howard, "Lessons of the Cold War," *Survival* 36, no. 4 (winter 1994–95): 166.

21. Oberdorfer, "Glaspie Says Saddam Is Guilty of Deception," A23.

22. See Jeffrey Record, "Defeating Desert Storm (and Why Saddam Didn't)", *Comparative Strategy* 12, no. 2 (April–June 1993): 127–28. See also Alexander George, *Forceful Persuasion* (Washington, D.C.: U.S. Institute Of Peace, 1991), 61–63.

Although the evidence about Iraqi intentions and decision-making in the Gulf war remains sketchy, it at least suggests that U.S. policies of deterrence both failed and succeeded: the effort to deter Saddam from invading Kuwait failed because of Saddam's mistaken evaluation of U.S. will; and the clear U.S. effort to use implicit nuclear retaliatory threats to deter Iraqi use of WMD appears to have been successful. This observation brings us back to the questions of interest. Can a policy of deterrence "work" in the second nuclear age? The Gulf war experience offers a recent answer that indeed it can, especially when backed by nuclear threats. Yet, which U.S. deterrence effort in the Gulf war is likely to be more reflective of the second nuclear age: the apparent success or the initial failure? Perhaps the Gulf war provides us with the lesson that we can expect both success and failure from policies of deterrence, and that we may not know which to expect on any given occasion.

Chapter 3 demonstrated the continuing tremendous confidence that U.S. officials and expert commentators have in nuclear deterrence policies. To repeat the recent claim by Jan Lodal, principal deputy undersecretary of defense for policy: "Nuclear deterrence worked throughout the Cold War, it continues to work now, it will work into the future . . . the exact same kinds of nuclear deterrence calculations that have always worked will continue to work."[23] Such claims clearly are born of decades of confidence that, as Harold Brown observed more than a decade earlier, deterrence policy should be made "conclusive" against the possibilities of mistake or folly by the proper application of nuclear threats.

Mistakes

Can U.S. deterrence policies for the second nuclear age be made reliable through the mechanism suggested by the Assured Vulnerability paradigm—getting the nuclear threat right? In theory, it should be possible to establish policies of deterrence that

---

23. Jan Lodal (P)DUSD, Ashton Carter ASD (International Security Policy), with selected reporters, 31 July 1995, Washington, D.C., Press Conference Transcript, 9–10 (mimeographed).

we know to be "conclusive" vis-à-vis a rational challenger. To do so, however, would require not only that the challenger be a well-informed, rational, and sensible decision-maker, but that we be nearly omniscient. Consequently, we should not expect our deterrence policies to be "conclusive" in practice: despite the repeated, confident, and continuing statements from U.S. officials, deterrence cannot be "ensured."

Historically, policies of deterrence have failed for many different reasons.[24] For example, as described in Chapter 3, leaders have been grossly mistaken about the likely behavior of their opponents because they have misunderstood the opponent's determination, intent, goals, and/or capabilities. And opponents have operated from hierarchies of value so mutually unfamiliar that their respective actions appeared unreasonable, even irrational. Challengers have been driven by domestic conditions so intolerable that they were highly motivated to alter the status quo, to the point of being impervious to any practicable deterrence pressures. Leaders have been so uncomprehending of the crises and/or so limited in their decision-making capabilities by various psychological and cognitive factors, that they could not respond to the crisis in an adequately rational manner.

The failures of deterrence policies resulting from these factors do not reflect a failure of deterrence theory, as is suggested by

---

24. For a good selection of empirical studies using historical case studies to examine the success and failure of deterrence threats and policies, see Alexander George and Richard Smoke, *Deterrence in American Foreign Policy* (New York: Columbia Univ. Press, 1974); Lebow and Stein, *We All Lost the Cold War*; Richard Lebow, *Between Peace and War* (Baltimore: Johns Hopkins Univ. Press, 1981); Robert Jervis, Richard Ned Lebow, and Janice Gross Stein, eds., *Psychology and Deterrence* (Baltimore: Johns Hopkins Univ. Press, 1985); Richard Ned Lebow and Janice Gross Stein, *When Does Deterrence Succeed And How Do We Know* (Ottawa, Ontario: Canadian Institute for International Peace and Security, 1990); Donald Kagan, *On the Origins of War* (New York: Doubleday, 1995); Peter Karsten, Peter Howell, and Artis Allen, *Military Threats* (Westport, Conn.: Greenwood, 1984); Paul Huth and Bruce Russett, "What Makes Deterrence Work?" *World Politics* 36, no. 4 (July 1984): 496–526; Gordon Craig and Alexander George, *Force and Statecraft*, 3d ed. (New York: Oxford Univ. Press, 1995); Alex Roberto Hybel, *Power over Rationality* (Albany: State Univ. of New York Press, 1993); Alexander George, *Forceful Persuasion* (Washington, D.C.: U.S. Institute of Peace, 1991); Elli Lieberman, *Deterrence Theory: Success or Failure in Arab-Israeli Wars?*(Washington, D.C.: Institute for National Strategic Studies, National Defense University, 1995); Paul K. Huth, *Extended Deterrence and the Prevention of War* (New Haven: Yale Univ. Press, 1988); Paul Davis and John Arquilla, *Deterring or Coercing Opponents in Crisis* (Santa Monica, Calif.: RAND, 1995); and Barry Wolf, *When the Weak Attack the Strong: Failures of Deterrence*, N-3261-A (Santa Monica, Calif.: RAND, 1991).

some of the best in the field.[25] Recall that deterrence theory posits that a rational challenger will be deterred from an action when it calculates that the costs of the action as threatened by the deterrer will outweigh the benefits. Deterrence theory does not stipulate that leaders always will calculate rationally, act sensibly, be fully informed about their situation or their opponent. Nor does it promise that very potent threats backed by unquestioned resolve will be sufficient to deter when the challenger is so highly motivated that it is willing to run high risks and accept high costs. Deterrence theory essentially describes a decision-making process, including the conditions it stipulates are necessary for the challenger to behave as predicted. Yet these conditions are to be hoped for, not assumed; they will not be present in all cases and should not be expected to be present in all cases. As the Group for the Advancement of Psychiatry has observed with regard to deterrence theory, "It rests on certain dubious psychological assumptions."[26]

When the conditions stipulated by the theory are not met, policies of deterrence should not be expected to work predictably. The challenger may not pursue the proscribed provocation in any event. Such occasions, however, do not represent deterrence success and cannot serve as the basis for confidence in policies. When deterrers or challengers are not calculating rationally, are poorly informed or mistaken about the opponent or situation, or when challengers are too highly motivated to be deterred by even potent threats, deterrence theory has not failed or been shown in error. The participants simply are operating outside the boundaries stipulated in deterrence theory. When policies of deterrence fail as a result of such factors, the error is in the expectation of the policy working when the theory is not applicable.

The expectations associated with Assured Vulnerability—that U.S. commitments will be judged credible, that challengers will be

<hr />

25. For example, Lebow and Stein observe that "deterrence failures that occur when resolve is unquestioned and capability potent, represent failures of deterrence theory . . . faulty estimates that are wildly at variance with available information contradict the most important assumption of deterrence theory: that leaders behave more or less in accord with rational norms." Lebow and Stein, *When Does Deterrence Succeed and How Do We Know?* 56.

26. Group for the Advancement of Psychiatry, Committee on Social Issues, *Psychiatric Aspects of the Prevention of Nuclear War*, Report no. 57 (September 1964), 268.

generically rational and reasonable, and consequently that deterrence policy will work if we can just wield the proper threat—have been a fundamental, if largely unrecognized, problem in normative analyses of U.S. deterrence policy. In most Cold War analyses of strategic deterrence "stability," those factors associated with the character of the challenger and the context that can render deterrence unreliable simply were ignored or not taken into serious consideration:[27] military capabilities are compared, strategic exchanges are modeled, and net war outcomes projected. If, based on the result of force exchange analysis, it appears that net costs (in terms of targets destroyed) would be unacceptable to the attacker, deterrence is assumed to be "stable." If an acceptable level of damage is anticipated, or even a *net* gain in a crisis, then an incentive to strike is presumed and the condition is considered "unstable."

Such force exchange analyses have long been employed to draw conclusions about the "stabilizing" or "destabilizing" effect of changes in the U.S. strategic force posture. That is, conclusions

---

27. The classic case is the analysis of strategic deterrence stability and its requirements that supported the McNamara concept of "Assured Destruction": deterrence stability is equated to a particular level of destructive potential and the forces necessary to inflict that destruction, with little or no reference to the character of the challenger or context. See Alain Enthoven and K. Wayne Smith, *How Much Is Enough?* (New York: Harper and Row, 1971), 207–10. As Fred Kaplan observes of such Assured Destruction calculations: "The idea was that as long as the Soviets knew that we could retaliate, that would deter them. McNamara's Whiz Kids calculated that the Soviets would be sufficiently deterred if we could kill 30 percent of their population and destroy half of their industrial capacity, and, further more, that this task could be accomplished with the explosive power of 400 megatons.

"It all appeared scientific and precise, but in fact it had little to do with any formulation of how much would be enough to deter the Soviets. It was the output of a computer program designed by Alain Enthoven, 'laying down' one-megaton bombs against Soviet cities and calculating, at various points, how much additional damage one additional bomb would do." Fred Kaplan, *The Wizards of Armageddon* (Stanford: Stanford Univ. Press, 1983), 317; see also 318–19.

A few of the numerous more recent examples in which contextual factors are wholly or largely absent are Glenn Kent and David Thaler, *First-Strike Stability: A Methodology for Evaluating Strategic Forces*, R-3765-AF (Santa Monica, Calif.: RAND, August 1989); Glenn A. Kent, Randall J. DeValk, and David E. Thaler, *A Calculus of First-Strike Stability (A Criterion for Evaluating Strategic Forces)*, RAND Note, N-2526-AF (Santa Monica, Calif.: RAND, June 1988); Paul L. Chrzanowski, "Transition to Deterrence Based on Strategic Defense," *Energy and Technology Review* (January–February 1987): 31–45; Kenneth Watman and Dean Wilkening, *Strategic Defenses and First-Strike Stability*, R-3412-FF/RC (Santa Monica, Calif.: RAND, November 1986); C. Max et al., *Deployment Stability of Strategic Defenses*, JSR-85-926 (McLean, Va.: JASON, Mitre Corp., October 1986); Roy Radner, "A Model of Defense-Protected Build Down," in, *Strategic Defenses and Arms Control*, Alvin M. Weinberg and Jack N. Barkenbus, eds. (New York: Paragon House, 1988), 111–42; and Stephen O. Fought, *SDI: A Policy Analysis* (Newport, R.I.: Naval War College Press, 1987).

were offered concerning how a change in the strategic force balance would affect the stability of the U.S.-Soviet deterrence relationship. The assumption in such analysis, typically left unstated, was that political leaders would behave as the strategic equivalent of Adam Smith's "economic man." Leaders are assumed to be ready, willing, and able to engage in well-informed and rational cost-benefit calculations and to make their decisions accordingly. They are assumed to be knowledgeable, cognizant of opponents' political interests, values, intentions, and military capabilities, able to absorb information, and able to implement benefit-maximizing/cost-minimizing decisions under great stress. This assumption that a political leader will be a rational, informed "strategic man" is a convenience; it allows conclusions to be drawn about the probability of war based almost exclusively on that which is relatively easy to do: compare strategic force capabilities and model strategic force exchanges.

To base deterrence policy recommendations on this convenient assumption, however, was to mistakenly regard abstract theory as an adequate guide for specific policy application. Despite its convenience, this approach cannot serve as the basis for specific policy application. It does not incorporate any of the key contextual factors—the possibility for mistakes, misperceptions, ignorance, under- or unrecognized motivation, will, and values— and does not take into account how these factors can shape the challenger's decision-making.[28] Alexander George's observation about the attribution of rationality to the challenger in coercive strategies is equally valid for policies of deterrence: "The assumption of rationality does not suffice to make a confident prediction as to what an opponent will do when subjected, as Saddam Hussein was, to an ultimatum. . . . . The assumption of rationality on which the strategy of coercive diplomacy relies must somehow take into account psychological, cultural, and political variables that can affect the opponent's response to an ultimatum."[29]

---

28. Alexander George rightly identifies this problem as equally valid for strategies of coercive diplomacy. See *Forceful Persuasion*, 4.

29. Ibid, 62.

Classic discussions of strategic deterrence focused on two requirements for an effective deterrence policy: the capability to inflict unacceptable damage (variously defined) and the manifest intent behind that threat. Seminar discussions of deterrence typically begin with the well-worn axiom that deterrence is a function of the capability and credibility of the threat. Yet these well-known requirements are not sufficient for deterrence to "work." As noted above, an entire set of oft-ignored but necessary conditions must contribute to the decision-making process on both (or all) sides if deterrence policies are to function as envisaged. These include leaders capable of relatively unbiased assessments of information and realistic linkage of actions to consequences; political systems permitting the implementation of rational decisions as policy; leaders who are well informed and comprehend the intentions, interests, commitments, and values of the opponent(s); leaders who focus on external factors (that is, competing military capabilities) as the final determinant of decisions; and leaders who understand the military capabilities and consequences involved in their decisions, at least at a general level.

If one or several of these conditions are absent, there is no basis for assuming that the necessary cost-benefit calculations could be conducted predictably, would determine policy, and/or could have useful deterrent effect. The prospective existence and weight of these psychological/political conditions is difficult to identify and measure for any specific case; hence the overwhelming tendency to ignore them and base grandiose conclusions about deterrence on a piece of the puzzle that is most easily calculated, that is, the nuclear threats.

When deterrence is defined only in terms of maintaining a particular level of military capability relative to an opponent and the contextual factors are ignored, then it is not difficult to conclude that stability is relatively "easy" to calculate and predict: in the U.S. strategic debate, the maintenance of survivable nuclear retaliatory forces was equated with deterrence stability. But, if the necessary political/psychological factors discussed above are acknowledged as important in decision-making, then the now-traditional U.S. stability analyses must be recognized as inherently inadequate as the basis for specific policy application—regardless of the "strategic balance"—because the convenient assumption about political decision-makers as "strategic man" does not reliably reflect reality.

There is nothing wrong if, as an intellectual exercise, one posits "countries A and B," assumes that "strategic man" is at the helm of each, calculates force exchanges, and then draws conclusions about the stability of the deterrence relationship for countries A and B. The problem is that the practitioners of such deterrence analyses have tended to forget that they had created a fictitious world and have claimed that their conclusions are valid for the real world of international relations. It should not be considered quibbling to note that there is no country A or B on the U.N. roster, and on some occasions "strategic man" will not be at the helm of those countries that do exist. A large grain of salt should be taken with any claims about deterrence that so ignore the character of the opponents and context. As Fred Iklé, former U.S. undersecretary of defense for policy, has noted, "In the real world, nuclear forces are built and managed not by two indistinguishable 'sides,' but by very distinct governments and military organizations. These, in turn, are run by people, people who are ignorant of many facts, people who can be gripped by anger or fear, people who make mistakes—sometimes dreadful mistakes."[30]

Serious students of deterrence have for years recognized the potential shortcoming of deterrence theory as the basis for predicting the actual behavior of leaders and the outcome of deterrence policies, and have expressed proper warnings about confident claims and expectations extrapolated from deterrence theory.[31] Similarly, many students of international conflict have

---

30. Fred Charles Iklé, "Nuclear Strategy: Can There Be a Happy Ending?" *Foreign Affairs* 63, no. 4 (spring 1985): 10.

31. As Alexander George and Richard Smoke observed: "The unitary actor, rationality, and the other assumptions and simplifications we have discussed are necessary ones to make manageable the logical tracing out of abstract [deterrence] theory. So long as it is kept clearly in mind that deterrence theory does have an abstract-deductive character, they are harmless enough.

"The hazard begins to enter in when this simplified model is used in a normative-prescriptive mode. . . . Here we wish to emphasize the many respects in which current deterrence theory fails to satisfy the prerequisites of normative-prescriptive theory. Methodologically, deterrence theory simply has not been adequately tested against historical experiences. . . . Substantively, deterrence theory is seriously incomplete, to say

long warned against the temptation of basing analysis on country A and country B abstractions that assume countries to be "structurally alike in essence" and driven predictably by common unifying themes such as the survival of the state and the avoidance of war.[32] In seeking to understand the "nature of modern warfare," for example, professor Adda Bozeman suggested guidance for the twentieth century that is likely to be even more important for understanding deterrence in the twenty-first: "In the multicultural environment of the twentieth century, foreign-policymakers must recognize and analyze multiple, distinct cultures as well as political systems that differ from each other significantly in their modes of rational and normative thought, their value orientation, and their dispositions in foreign affairs. . . . The evidence shows, in particular, that [in contrast to Western thought] peace is neither the dominant value nor the norm in foreign relations and that war, far from being perceived as immoral or abnormal, is viewed positively."[33]

Yet U.S. officials and commentators have ignored these fair warnings in their confident claims, in the absence of any serious reference to contextual factors, that nuclear deterrence policies can be "ensured," can be made "conclusive." Their assumption of a generically rational and sensible opponent, which must be the basis for such confidence, may be worse than simply unhelpful. It may be misleading, producing policy prescriptions based on a fictitious construct, and as likely to provoke as to deter.

At a minimum, to have confidence that a deterrence policy would be "conclusive," it would have to be informed as to the type of threat necessary given the challenger's interests, motivations and will, and the measures necessary to make that threat sufficiently understood and credible—to be decisive in the challenger's decision-making. The deterrer would have to know to whom and how the threat should be communicated to be effective, and of course the challenger would have to be a rational deci-

---

the least for a normative-prescriptive application." George and Smoke, *Deterrence in American Foreign Policy*, 82–83.

32. For example, see the discussion by Adda Bozeman, "War and the Clash of Ideas," *Orbis* 20, no. 1 (spring 1976): 76.

33. Ibid., 102.

sion-maker and sensible according to the deterrer's understanding. In short, the deterrer must be extremely knowledgeable about both the challenger and the context of the crisis and must orchestrate its policy according to the specific requirements presented by that challenger and context.

The implications of this for U.S. deterrence policies in the second nuclear age are significant. Most obviously, U.S. leaders and commentators should not engage in gross generalizations about deterrence or base their expectations on the military balance alone. Rather, they must try to target their policies to the particular context and character of the opponent: "No study of threats . . . could succeed in giving to a national leadership any more than some ideas as to 'what mattered' or how to proceed, given certain circumstances. None of these ideas, moreover, would supplant the particular conditions that prevail in any threat environment, independently of how deftly one manages the crisis. That is to say, if one does not threaten the right target for the right reasons, it may not matter how well one does it."[34]

Unfortunately, knowing with confidence what is the "right" threat, the "right" reasons, and the "right" target with regard to a particular adversary (as opposed to simply assuming a generically rational and sensible foe) may be very difficult. As Richard Lebow and Janice Stein conclude based on their historical case studies: "The strategy of deterrence makes unrealistic assumptions about the way people reason. . . . Human beings are not always instrumentally rational and are even less likely to be so in acute crises when they are emotionally aroused and confront intense conflict among their objectives. Yet this is precisely the situation in which defenders most rely on deterrence. The policy-making environment is also far from transparent. Cultural, political and personal barriers to assessment frequently combine to make it opaque to outsiders."[35] Indeed, U.S. leaders are unlikely to be sufficiently knowledgeable vis-à-vis many of the possible regional challengers of the second nuclear age to establish deterrence policies worthy

---

34. Karsten, Howell, and Allen, *Military Threats*, xii. Huth and Russett conclude that "a definition of deterrence as primarily sensitive to strict calculation of military capability is both mistaken and profoundly dangerous." "What Makes Deterrence Work?" 524.

35. Lebow and Stein, *We All Lost the Cold War*, 330–31.

of great confidence. And when policies of deterrence deserving of confidence have been established, we may not know that such is the case until after a crisis plays itself out—if then.

Yet the Assured Vulnerability paradigm's overwhelming focus on the configuration of the nuclear threat as the determinant of deterrence effectiveness has promoted a continuing confidence among U.S. officials and commentators that as long as we can threaten to "turn you into a sea of radioactive glass," as John Pike puts it, the challenger—any challenger—will be deterred. This now-venerable notion is suspect, as are the confident claims based on it.

It appears that "fearsome" capabilities may, to some extent, compensate for a possible deficit in the challenger's view of the deterrer's will.[36] And it seems likely that under some conditions nuclear threats will increase the credibility of a deterrence policy that, if limited to conventional threats, would fail.[37] As discussed above, this may have been the case with Saddam Hussein and the deterrence of Iraqi WMD use in the Gulf war. Policies of deterrence, however, can fail for reasons that are not amenable to correction even by the fearsomeness of nuclear threats because the introduction of nuclear weapons cannot remove the human capacity to be ignorant, to behave unpredictably or irrationally, and/or to make profound mistakes.[38] As Albert Einstein observed,

---

36. As Kenneth Watman and Dean Wilkening conclude based on their empirical investigation, "The communication of a strong will to act can compensate to some extent for a less certain military capability. Similarly, a fearsome military capability can compensate for some uncertainty the adversary may feel about the U.S. will to act." *U.S. Regional Deterrence Strategies* (Santa Monica, Calif.: RAND, 1995), 57.

37. Ibid, 8–9.

38. See the discussion in Karsten, Howell, and Allen, *Military Threats*, 85. And, as Lebow concludes, "Technology has wrought astounding changes in our lives . . . but there is no evidence that mankind itself has become better able to regulate its individual or collective destinies. It is a truism that the complexity of the modern world and the devastating power of nuclear weapons demand more sophisticated and 'rational' approaches to decision-making. Yet, recent experience gives no indication that contemporary political leaders are any more effective than their predecessors in regulating conflict and eschewing violence. Nor do they appear to reach decisions in a more rational manner. . . . Evidence is accumulating to the effect that people are on the whole incapable of carrying out the mental operations required by such a dispassionate and logical approach to policy-making. Unfortunately, the range of decision-making pathologies that afflicted, say, the Japanese and American governments in 1941 and European statesmen in 1914 or for that matter the ancient Athenians and Spartans continue to plague contemporary political elites." Lebow, *Between Peace and War*, 17–18.

"The unleashed power of the atom has changed everything except our ways of thinking."

The advent of nuclear weapons did introduce the unique possibility of geographically widespread and very rapid destruction. Many suggest, in line with Assured Vulnerability, that this unique severity of nuclear threats should now make deterrence reliable, even if it was not in the prenuclear period. Yet, the differences between the nuclear age and the past in this regard, particularly the perceived differences, may not be so significant. While the actual possibility of widespread and rapid destruction is new, its expectation is not. Leaders in the past have expected then-modern military means to be so destructive as to threaten civilization if ever used. And, of course, the prospect of rapid societal annihilation on a localized basis has confronted leaders for thousands of years. The utter destruction of Carthage by Rome at the conclusion of the Third Punic War, the taking of Abydos by Philip V in 200 B.C., the fate of Russian princes before the Mongol invasions, and Caesar's total annihilation of the Usipetes and Tencteri Germanic tribes in 55 B.C. are just a few of the many examples illustrating this point.

Historically, the utter destruction of entire cities by military force did take place with some regularity. In 1240, for example, Mongol warriors under Subudai Bahadur crossed the frozen Dnieper River to arrive at the gates of the great stone-walled city of Kiev. Despite a gallant defense, Kiev was torched and the population was massacred. The destruction of Kiev was so ferocious that six years later the city remained in near-complete ruins and the ground was littered with "countless skulls and bones of dead men." Similarly, Subudai's earlier destruction of Riazan was so complete that "no eyes remained open to weep for the dead."[39] In short, leaders in the past have known or believed that their decisions would affect the probability of utter societal destruction, at least for them and their society, but that prospect did not render threats thereof reliable instruments for deterrence or coercion.[40]

---

39. See Richard Gabriel and Donald Boose Jr., *The Great Battles of Antiquity* (Westport, Conn.: Greenwood, 1994), 530–31.

40. Thucydides, for example, reports that in 416 B.C. the islanders of Melos were presented with a credible Athenian threat of annihilation as part of the Athenian bid to gain Melian allegiance in the Second Peloponnesian War. The Melians resisted, trusting "in

In more recent cases, leaders have expected conventional war to involve the type of destruction we now associate with nuclear war. For example, as mentioned earlier, in the 1930s the British political elite anticipated that air warfare would be similar to what we now anticipate of nuclear warfare. A comment very instructive in this regard comes from former British Prime Minister Harold Macmillan's memoirs: "Among other deterrents of war in 1938, expert advice had indicated that bombing of London and the great cities would lead to casualties of the order of hundreds of thousands or even millions within a few weeks. We thought of air warfare in 1939 rather as people think of nuclear warfare today."[41] Indeed, a concept of mutual deterrence emerged in British writings during the 1930s that is strikingly similar to current concepts of mutual nuclear deterrence. The notion, of course, was that mutual expectations of the destruction resulting from then-modern air power, "a horror unparalleled in the grim annals of war," would serve to deter war. As a British 1938 text on air power demonstrates, the mutual potential for air attack was thought to hold the prospect for mutual deterrence.

> The very magnitude of the disaster that is possible may prove to be a restraining influence. Because the riposte is certain, because it cannot be parried, a belligerent will think twice and again before he initiates a mode of warfare the final outcome of which is incalculable. The deterrence influence may, indeed, be greater than that. It may tend to prevent not only raids on cities but resort to war in any shape or form. . . .

> At present air attack is regarded as a menace, a withheld thunderbolt, an impending calamity. All nations fear it. For

---

fortune." The Athenians killed the men, sold the women and children into slavery, and colonized the island themselves. See *The Peloponnesian War* (New York: Random House, 1951), 330–37.

41. Harold Macmillian, *Winds of Change, 1914–1939* (London: Macmillan, 1966), 575. See the discussion of British concerns about the German bomber threat in Uri Bialer, *The Shadow of the Bomber: The Fear of Air Attack and British Politics* (London: Royal Historical Society, 1980), 158.

the very reason it should be a deterrent influence against war.[42]

Clearly, the expectation of rapid and widespread devastation is not new to the nuclear age, nor is the hope that mutual deterrence would result from that expectation.[43]

The expectation that nuclear threats, manipulated as necessary, can render deterrence "conclusive" toward a sensible opponent is similar to the view popularized in Britain just prior to World War I by Norman Angell's *The Great Illusion*: then-modern economic conditions and interdependence should make war unthinkable for sensible leaders because the economic cost, even to the victor, would not be worth the price of war.[44]

Angell's thesis undoubtedly was at least partially true for most of the players in World War I. For Britain, a "victor," the cost of World War I was in fact enormous. Nevertheless, the fact that war *should* generally have been anticipated as too costly did not keep the peace in 1914. British leaders ultimately judged war to be preferable to the type of peace expected in the absence of war. The modern nuclear-based variant of Angell's position suggests that nuclear threats should establish a basic floor of reliability for deterrence policies because the threat is so severe. As Robert Jervis notes concerning the anticipated effect of nuclear threats, "if decisionmakers are 'sensible,' peace is the most likely outcome."[45]

One would hope Jervis's thesis to be valid. Yet, the introduction of nuclear weapons has not brought an end to the capacity of leaders to have poor judgment, to base their actions on faulty assumptions, or to make mistakes—to not be "sensible" as defined by their opponent. Neither have nuclear weapons necessarily increased the degree of mutual understanding, knowledge, empa-

---

42. J.M. Spaight, *Air Power in the Next War* (London: Geoffrey Bles, 1938), 126.

43. See George Quester, "Deterrence before Hiroshima: The Past as Prologue," in *The Search for Strategy*, ed. Gary Guertner (Westport, Conn.: Greenwood, 1993), 113–46.

44. Norman Angell, *The Great Illusion*, 4th ed. (New York: Knickerbocker, 1913). Barbara Tuchman reports that Angell's book and thesis had an important impact on British thinking about the likelihood of war prior to World War I. See Tuchman, *The Guns of August* (New York: Dell, 1962), 24–25.

45. Robert Jervis, "The Political Effects of Nuclear Weapons: A Comment," *International Security* 13, no. 2 (fall 1988): 81.

thy, rationality, and reasonableness with which leaders approach issues of war, peace, and brinksmanship: leaders in the past have either incorrectly anticipated nuclearlike levels of destruction, or they have correctly anticipated the possibility that they and their society could be destroyed utterly. Whether leaders' expectations of vast destruction proved to be accurate or exaggerated, in neither case did such expectations render deterrence reliable. In short, there is ample reason to doubt the widespread notion that, in contrast to the past, nuclear weapons "have changed everything," permitting confidence that deterrence policies can now be made "conclusive."[46]

How Deterrence Policies Fail

Following is an accounting of some of the factors that can lead to the failure of deterrence policies, whether because leaders operate outside the boundaries assumed in deterrence theory or because policies of deterrence are applied mistakenly, inappropriately, or clumsily. Historical references are presented for illustrative purposes.[47] The most obvious example of leaders who operate outside

---

46. Donald Kagan's study of the Cuban missile crisis moved him to the same conclusion. See Kagan, *On the Origins of War*, 9. In the detailed analysis by Karsten, Howell, and Allen, an analysis combining historical case study and quantitative social science methods, the distinctions between the working of threat for deterrence and coercion before and after World War II are found to be modest, with the same contextual factors determining the success or failure of a threat in both. The authors' conclusion is important to this discussion: "The possession of nuclear weapons by both a threatener and a target in some of today's threats means (one hopes) that both parties sense that neither can truly 'win.' . . . This same sense of the possibility of self-destruction was felt by threatener (Lord Grey) and target (the Kaiser) in 1914, and by another English threatener (Neville Chamberlain) in 1938 and 1939. The rubble might not 'bounce,' but 'civilization as we know it' would end just the same. We would do well to recall in particular the tragic vision of Grey and Kaiser Wilhelm, a vision that did not lead Europe back from the brink of that devastating war. Their vision of the cost did not prevent its payment. Nor can threats today rely on high costs for their success or peaceful resolution." *Military Threats*, 85. In the fifty-four cases examined, Huth and Russett found that "only a marginal contribution [to deterrence] was made by the possession of nuclear weapons." "What Makes Deterrence Work?" 523.

47. These historical illustrations are derived from a large number of case studies I began pursuing in 1979, some of which I have included in several earlier published works. See, for example, Keith Payne, *Nuclear Deterrence in U.S.-Soviet Relations* (Boulder, Colo.: Westview, 1982), 97–111; Keith Payne and Lawrence Fink, "Deterrence without Defense: Gambling on Perfection," *Strategic Review* 17, no. 1 (winter 1989): 25–40; and Keith Payne, "Munich Fifty Years After," in, *The Meaning of Munich Fifty Years Later*, ed. Kenneth Jensen and David Wurmser (Washington, D.C.: U.S. Institute of Peace, 1990), 57–68. In addition, I also have drawn on some of the excellent and now-substantial case-study work by those

the boundaries of deterrence theory and cannot be expected to behave predictably in a deterrence relationship are those who are so disabled by psychopathy that they cannot be expected to engage consistently in rational decision-making.[48] Such leaders appear to be the type Secretary of Defense Perry identified in his warning about deterrence in the second nuclear age (presented in Chapter 3): "The bad news is that in this era, deterrence may not provide even the cold comfort it did during the Cold War. We may be facing terrorists or rogue regimes with ballistic missiles and nuclear weapons at the same time in the future, and they may not buy into our deterrence theory. Indeed, they may be madder than 'MAD.'"[49]

Fortunately, the incidences of leaders so disabled by psychopathy, while not unprecedented historically, appear to be relatively rare. One historical review of the subject indicates, for example, that at least seventy-five chiefs of state over the past four centuries have suffered severe mental disturbances during their tenure, including England's Henry VI and George III, Ludwig II of Bavaria, and Adolf Hitler.[50] Secretary Perry's warning about "rogue" leaders who are "madder than MAD" may, in particular, reflect the finding of some analyses that the frequently unstable and violent political environment of developing countries facilitates the emergence of leaders with paranoid personalities.[51]

Soviet leader Josef Stalin certainly appears to fit such a description. The extremes of his leadership indicate the possibility of

---

seeking to examine the causes of war or to test deterrence theory in the laboratory of history, including Alexander George, Richard Smoke, Richard Lebow, Janice Stein, Paul Huth, Alex Hybel, Peter Karsten, and, most recently, Donald Kagan, John Stossinger, Elli Lieberman, Kenneth Watman, Dean Wilkening, Paul Davis, and John Arquilla.

48. Leaders so disabled could not be predicted to engage even in the less exacting standards of "rational choice theory." For a discussion of "rational choice theory" in deterrence, see Watman and Wilkening *Strategic Defenses and First-Strike Stability*, 16–18.

49. Secretary of Defense William J. Perry, *On Ballistic Missile Defense: Excerpt from a Speech to the Chicago Council on Foreign Relations*, 8 March 1995, 1 (mimeographed).

50. See Robert Noland, "Presidential Disability and the Proposed Constitutional Amendment," *American Psychologist* 21, no. 3 (March 1966): 232. See also Jonathan M. Roberts, *Decision-Making during International Crises* (New York: St. Martin's, 1988), 186; Wolf, *When the Weak Attack the Strong: Failures of Deterrence*, 7–8, 16; and, Watman and Wilkening, *U.S. Regional Deterrence Strategies*, 24–26.

51. See Robert Tucker, "The Dictator and Totalitarianism," in *A Source Book for the Study of Personality and Politics*, ed. Fred Greenstein and Michael Lerner (Chicago: Markham, 1971), 469–70.

psychopathy, and at least some of his colleagues have since identified him as paranoid and compulsive. Nikita Khrushchev quotes Stalin as stating, "I trust no one, not even myself," and then comments:

> This was a shocking admission. We had seen this mistrust of people for a long time, but now he was acknowledging it himself, and so categorically. Can you imagine such a statement coming from a man who decided the fate of his country and influenced the fate of the world? It's one thing not to trust people. That was his right, even if his extreme mistrust did indicate that he had a serious psychological problem. But it's another thing when a man is compulsively driven to eliminate anyone he doesn't trust. . . . Every year it became more and more obvious that Stalin was weakening mentally as well as physically.

Khrushchev, adds, "In my opinion it was during the war that Stalin started to be not quite right in the head."[52]

It is interesting to note that Khrushchev pinpoints World War II as the time frame for the emergence of Stalin's possible mental disturbances. Stalin's behavior at the outset of the 1941 German invasion of the Soviet Union under Operation Barbarossa and immediately thereafter frequently is identified as involving a mental breakdown of some order.[53] His refusal to acknowledge hostile German military intentions in the face of abundant evidence and even after the invasion had begun indicates that Stalin may have been operating outside the behavioral assumptions of deterrence theory. During the spring of 1941, reports from Soviet military commanders at the border and from the Soviet embassy in Berlin warned of an impending German invasion.[54] Not only did Stalin ignore such reports and deny the possibility, but Soviet comman-

---

52. Nikita Khrushchev, *Khrushchev Remembers*, ed. and trans. Strobe Talbott (Boston: Little, Brown, 1970), 307, 311.

53. See, for example, Edward Crankshaw's comment in, ibid., 166.

54. For example, a report submitted by Soviet diplomats in Berlin to Moscow in May 1941 warned that a German attack against the Soviet Union could be expected at any moment. See Valentin Berzhkov, *S diplomaticheskoi missievi v Berlin 1940–1941 Tegeran 1943* (Tashkent: Iadatel'stvo Uzbekistan, 1971), 52.

ders issuing them were reprimanded and denounced as provocateurs.

In addition, recently released documents from Russian archives indicate that Stalin encouraged a hesitating Chinese leader, Mao Zedong, to intervene with five or six divisions on behalf of North Korea in 1950, promising Soviet fidelity to China even if the latter's intervention led to World War III. Stalin displayed a willingness "for high-stakes gambling which was fraught with the potential for global disaster." In his communiqué to Mao, for example, Stalin stated, "If a war [with the U.S.] is inevitable, then let it be waged now."[55] This does not, of course, necessarily demonstrate psychopathy; it does, nevertheless, demonstrate that in his discussions with Mao, Stalin had transcended the bounds of sensibility, as understood in Washington.

More recently, there is some indication that Saddam Hussein suffered from a personality disorder called "malignant narcissism" which may have affected his decision-making prior to and during the Gulf war. Malignant narcissism is "a dangerous personality disorder characterized by extreme grandiosity, paranoia, sadistic cruelty, and a total lack of remorse."[56] This assessment of Hussein was offered in the personality profile developed by Jerrold Post, formerly of the CIA's Center for the Analysis of Personality and Political Behavior, and circulated to senior U.S. officials during the Gulf crises. Post described Hussein as "psychologically in touch with reality" but "often politically out of touch with reality. . . . It is this political personality constellation—messianic ambition for unlimited power, absence of conscience, unconstrained aggression, and a paranoid outlook—that make Saddam Hussein so dangerous."[57]

---

55. See the excellent recent work by Russian scholar Alexandre Mansourov, "Stalin, Mao, Kim, and China's Decision to Enter the Korean War, September 16–October 15, 1950: New Evidence from the Russian Archives," *Cold War International History Project Bulletin*, nos. 6–7 (winter 1995–96): 101.

56. See the discussion of the intelligence community's personality profiles of Saddam Hussein in Thomas Amsted, "Psychology and the CIA: Leaders on the Couch," *Foreign Policy*, no. 95 (summer 1994): 112–13.

57. Jerrold Post's psychological profile of Saddam Hussein is presented in U.S. House, Committee on Armed Services, *Crisis in the Persian Gulf: Sanctions, Diplomacy and War: Hearings*, 101st Cong., 2d sess. (Washington, D.C.: GPO, 1991), 38–57; quotation from 48 and 50. In a personality profile the Israeli intelligence agency Mossad reportedly identified Saddam Hussein prior to the Gulf War as dangerous and suffering from extreme

It would be sheer speculation to suggest that this personality disorder affected Saddam to the extent of impeding rational decision-making. But it certainly could have contributed to behavior that was considered unreasonable in Washington. President Bush, for example, considered Hussein's behavior to be so aberrant that he suspected him of suffering from psychopathy, stating of Hussein, "Maybe you have to be personally . . . mad to make such crazy decisions."[58]

Psychopathy inhibiting the necessary rational decision-making process can be brought on by stress, which can be particularly acute in crises.[59] We know that in crisis situations, decisions tend to be based on fairly simplified cognitive structures that tend to reduce the range of options perceived by the leaders involved. Also, there is no doubt that objective rationality in decision-making can be impaired by various psychological defense mechanisms.[60] One example of the type of psychological factors that appears to have led rational leaders to such miscalculation is the *denial* mechanism. Denial can affect a person who is compelled to choose among a panoply of difficult options. A choice is made, and the decision-maker subsequently simply denies the possible negative consequences associated with the chosen course and ignores information suggesting negative consequences associated with that choice.

Denial is a basic human psychological reaction to danger and involves "various degrees of nonperception, nonrecognition, nonunderstanding, or nonacceptance of certain realities."[61] Detailed historical case studies demonstrate that this psychological defense mechanism has indeed been significant in miscalculations that resulted in the outbreak of crises and wars during both

---

mood swings. See, Andrew Meisels, "Israelis Say Handwriting Shows Saddam as Lunatic," *Washington Times*, 2 August 1990, A10.

58. See *A Gulf War Exclusive*, 7.

59. As detailed in Lebow and Stein, *We All Lost the Cold War*, 332–38.

60. For a basic discussion of psychological defense mechanisms such as repression and denial, see William N. Dember and James J. Jenkins, *General Psychology: Modeling Behavior and Experience* (Englewood Cliffs, N.J.: Prentice-Hall, 1970), 659–78; and Lee Roy Beach, *Psychology: Core Concepts and Special Topics* (New York: Holt, Rinehart and Winston, 1973), 187–98.

61. See Group for the Advancement of Psychiatry, Committee on Social Issues, *Psychiatric Aspects of the Prevention of Nuclear War*, 241.

the nuclear and the prenuclear ages.[62] Some statesmen have simply denied the strength of a foreign threat in the face of abundant information. This certainly was the cases with Stalin in 1941 and Saddam Hussein before and during Desert Storm. General Sammarai describes Saddam as "very reckless," simply dismissing out of hand any realistic assessment of U.S. military prowess.[63]

Another common psychological process important in this regard is *bolstering*.[64] This is the psychological tendency of decision-makers who are compelled to choose from several unsatisfying courses to select the least miserable, to minimize its possible negative consequences, and to exaggerate its positive attributes. The possibility for unwarranted overconfidence on the part of desperate leaders as a result of this psychological mechanism is obvious. As Richard Lebow observes, it blinds policymakers to the possible adverse consequences of their actions.[65]

A possible example of how psychological defense mechanisms and misperceptions of an opponent's likely behavior can impair decision-making may be demonstrated by Kaiser Wilhelm II's behavior in 1914. The kaiser hoped and believed that Britain would not participate in the Entente against Germany if the crisis between Germany's ally Austria-Hungary and Serbia—set in motion by the 1914 assassination of the Austrian archduke, Franz Ferdinand—escalated. He hoped and believed that Britain would at worst be neutral: this had become accepted wisdom in Berlin. On the calculation that a war could be so localized, and in loyalty to the assassinated archduke, Germany pressed Austria-Hungary toward an aggressive approach toward Serbia, and the kaiser issued a sacred pledge of support (*Nibelungentreue*) to Austria-

---

62. Karsten, Howell, and Allen, *Military Threats*, 21; Richard Lebow, "Miscalculation in the South Atlantic: The Origins of the Falklands War," in *Psychology and Deterrence*, ed. Jervis, Lebow, and Stein, 103, 119; and, in the same text, Lebow, "The Deterrence Deadlock: Is There a Way Out," 182–83.

63. See the statements by General Wafic Al Sammarai, in *Frontline*, "The Gulf War, Parts I and II," 9 and 10 January 1996. Comprehensive background interviews available via Internet Web site www.wgbh.org.

64. See the discussion in Lebow, *Between Peace and War*, 110.

65. Richard Lebow, "Miscalculation in the South Atlantic," 104.

Hungary.[66] Cables identifying Britain's likely involvement as a belligerent against Germany from the iconoclastic German ambassador in London, Prince Karl Max Litchnowsky, were edited and largely discounted until very late in July in favor of the accepted wisdom.

When, on 30 July, the kaiser no longer could deny the actual British direction in the now-boiling crisis, he appears to have been overcome with anxiety, despair, and bouts of aggressiveness. He spoke of holding the line, "whatever the cost,"[67] and wrote that evening of the coming conflict as if it had been forced upon him. He writes, as if in consolation for his pessimistic expectations for Germany, "If we are to bleed to death, England will at least lose India."[68] The kaiser's cognitive process and behavior do not appear to conform well to the specifications of deterrence theory, with its assumption of clearheaded, informed, and rational cost-benefit calculations. Nevertheless, the kaiser's behavior clearly helped to steer Germany's ill-fated course into World War I.

Another possible example of denial affecting decision-making involves the outbreak of the Russo-Japanese War of 1904. Tsar Nicholas clearly discounted Japanese expressions of concern regarding Russian expansion into Korea, in part because he simply denied the possibility that Japan, a non-European power, would dare to challenge Russia.[69] He held the Japanese in particular contempt, as did many of those providing him with advice on the dispute with Japan over Korea.[70] This view led the tsar to deny the possibility of a Japanese attack because it simply did not fit his disdainful view of Japan. When told of Japanese preparations for war by Kaiser Wilhelm II in November 1903, Tsar Nicholas reportedly replied that "there would be no war, because he did not wish it."[71] He appears to have felt at liberty to antagonize Japan by

---

66. See the discussion in John Stoessinger, *Why Nations Go to War* (New York, St. Martin's, 1993), 3–5.

67. Quoted in Karsten, Howell, and Allen, *Military Threats*, 12.

68. Quoted in Lebow, *Between Peace and War*, 144.

69. Count Sergei Witte, *The Memoirs of Count Witte*, ed. and trans. Abraham Yarmolinsky (Garden City, N.Y.: Doubleday, Page, 1921), 125.

70. Lebow, *Between Peace and War*, 76, 245–46.

71. Witte, *The Memoirs of Count Witte*, 125.

declaring the disputed areas of Port Arthur and territory on the Liaotung Peninsula a viceroyalty of the Russian Empire. Consequently, he was shocked by Japan's 6 February attack on Port Arthur, despite ample warnings of Japan's frustration with Russia's stalling in negotiations and a growing Japanese inclination to resolve the dispute militarily.

That these psychological defense mechanisms may impair a leader's otherwise rational decision-making illustrates the gap between the rational decision-making assumed in deterrence theory and the way factors not accounted for in that theory can affect decision-making.

Finally, of course, a leadership in the midst of a severe internal crisis may be incapable of reaching or effecting policy decisions that reflect a rational decision-making process. Recently, for example, the commander of U.S. forces in South Korea, General Gary Luck, stated that famine and political turmoil in North Korea was so desperate that "it is entirely possible that the leadership in Pyongyang is not or will not remain cohesive enough to make 'rational decisions.'"[72]

Deterrence policies also can fail as a result of miscalculations, misperceptions, and mistakes by deterrers and/or challengers who are fully capable of rational choice. A variety of factors can lead to this failing, but a fundamental problem is ignorance of the opponent, particularly of the opponent's value hierarchy. Understanding what the opponent values, and particularly how the opponent prioritizes values, is critical to identifying how it is likely to evaluate costs and benefits in a given situation, and the cost it will and will not be prepared to accept in pursuit of its goal. Understanding the opponent's value hierarchy, therefore, is critical to anticipating its likely determination and behavior under various deterrence conditions—particularly when that which the opponent values is under threat.[73] As Craig and George state, "It is often difficult to determine one's own national interests, let alone

72. As stated in General Luck's prepared statement before the House National Security Committee, 28 March 1996, transcript prepared by Federal News Service, 1–2.

73. For a treatment of this subject that continues to be of great value, see Stephen Maxwell, *Rationality in Deterrence*, Adelphi Papers, no. 50 (London: Institute For Strategic Studies, August 1968).

those of an opponent; but failure to do so can result in the disintegration of even the best deterrence strategy."[74]

A challenger may, for example, have goals that are unknown or considered "irrational" by the deterrer, and may be very highly motivated toward these goals. Yet, in establishing a reliable deterrence policy the deterrer must take the challenger's goals, high level of motivation, and determination into account. In fact, empirical studies of deterrence typically conclude that an understanding of these factors is extremely important in determining whether deterrence threats will succeed or fail.[75]

Unfortunately, as noted above, identifying a challenger's goals and the value it places on a disputed goal may be very difficult.[76] Such a large margin of error may be involved that the behavior expected of the opponent is grossly out of line with reality. This is particularly likely to be the case when the challenger's value hierarchy and goals are extreme by the deterrer's standards. Historically, highly motivated challengers are not uncommon, even in the United States: as American revolutionary Josiah Quincy (1744–75) proclaimed in *Observations on the Boston Port Bill* (the first of the British "Intolerable Acts"): "Blandishments will not fascinate us, nor will threats of a 'halter' intimidate, for, under God, we are determined that wheresoever, whensoever, or howsoever we shall be called to make our exit, we will die free men."[77]

Prior to the Gulf war, Saddam Hussein expressed statements that suggested a motivation, a value hierarchy, and a willingness to accept high risks and absorb great costs that were not appreciated by U.S. leaders:

If you use pressure, we will deploy pressure and force. We know that you can harm us, although we do not threaten

74. Craig and George, *Force and Statecraft*, 189.

75. See, for example, Karsten, Howell, and Allen, *Military Threats*, 63; Lebow and Stein, *When Does Deterrence Succeed and How Do We Know?* 3; Lebow and Stein, *We All Lost the Cold War*, 366; Watman and Wilkening, *U.S. Regional Deterrence Strategies*, 58; Paul K. Huth, *Extended Deterrence and the Prevention of War* (New Haven: Yale Univ. Press, 1986), 1, and Davis and Arquilla, *Deterring or Coercing Opponents*, 75–78.

76. For a discussion of the various sources of error in such an endeavor see Hybel, *Power over Rationality*, 36–37.

77. Quoted in Karsten, Howell, and Allen, *Military Threats*, 97.

you. But we too can harm you. . . . You can come to Iraq
with aircraft and missiles, but do not push us to the point
where we cease to care. And when we feel that you want
to injure our pride and take away the Iraqis' chance of a
high standard of living, then we will cease to care, and
death will be the choice for us. Then we would not care if
you fired 100 missiles for each missile we fired. Because
without pride life would have no value.[78]

Like the case in the Gulf war, historical cases demonstrate that
confusion about goals and determination frequently is the basis
for deterrence failure. When the challenger finds its existing
condition or direction to be intolerable, it will be prepared to take
great risks to alter that status quo. If the deterrer does not
appreciate the motivation animating the challenger and the
challenger's consequent level of determination, establishing
reliable policies of deterrence will be very difficult.

Even when the deterrer generally understands that the challenger is highly motivated to alter conditions it judges to be intolerable, to apply that knowledge and establish an effective deterrence policy may require very strong actions—and may be
impossible in practice. If the status quo is intolerable or the
opponent anticipates intolerable conditions, it may be "beyond
deterrence" for all practical purposes, despite the possibility of
identifying a theoretically effective deterrence policy. The initial
step for the deterrer, of course, is to be familiar with the
challenger's goals and value hierarchy and therefore to be in a
position to identify the opponent's will in a dispute.

The 1941 Japanese attack on Pearl Harbor represents another
case wherein the U.S. leadership was not sufficiently familiar with
the opponent's value hierarchy to understand its motivation;
effectively the opponent was "beyond deterrence." In this case,
U.S. leaders established a deterrent threat that was judged
credible by the Japanese leadership. But that leadership also
considered the compliance conditions established by the United

---

78. See Don Oberdorfer, "Missed Signals in the Middle East," *Washington Post
Magazine,* 17 March 1991, 39.

States to be wholly intolerable.[79] Misjudging the opponent's determination and yet posing a threat judged as severe in Tokyo, U.S. policies ultimately led Japan to a provocation that was acknowledged by Japanese leaders to be highly risky: Pearl Harbor.[80]

Japan appears to have recognized that the attack on Pearl Harbor represented a grave risk but calculated the slim prospect for an acceptable settlement to be preferable to the U.S. demand that it essentially withdraw from China and give up its goal of hegemony in Southeast Asia. Indeed, the classic historical analysis by the Office of the Chief of Military History, Department of the U.S. Army, concludes that Japanese leaders saw no alternative to war because they believed that Japan was "doomed" if it did not meet the U.S. challenge forcefully: "Japan had no alternative but to go to war while she still had the power to do so. She might lose, but defeat was better than humiliation and submission. 'Japan entered the war,' wrote a prince of the Imperial family, 'with a tragic determination and in desperate self-abandonment.' If she lost, 'there will be nothing to regret because she is doomed to collapse even without war.'"[81] Japanese leaders appear to have calculated rationally, but from a value hierarchy unfamiliar to American leaders; thus the Japanese motivation and path were contrary to Washington's expectations.

Ironically, the U.S. goal to deter and coerce Japan was undermined by the credibility of the U.S. threat. U.S. leaders assumed that Japan would be sensible, as they defined sensible, and not provoke war with a country clearly superior in military potential. But Japanese leaders were not calculating the costs and benefits of a highly risky attack versus those of an acceptable peace. Rather,

---

79. Because the U.S. oil embargo of Japan in 1941 was an attempt not simply to deter further Japanese aggression in Asia but also to coerce Japan to withdraw from China, this example is one involving U.S. attempts to deter and coerce. This distinction can be important, but the point to be illustrated here holds concerning the potential for deterrence or coercive threats to fail in the absence of an understanding of the opponent's value hierarchy.

80. For an excellent discussion of this case, see George, *Forceful Persuasion*, 19–23. See also Gordon W. Prange, *At Dawn We Slept* (New York: McGraw Hill, 1981); and John Toland, *The Rising Sun* (New York: Random House, 1970).

81. Louis Morton, "Japan's Decision for War," *Command Decisions* (New York: Harcourt, Brace, 1959), 87.

they focused on the type of peace that their compliance with the credible U.S. threat would provide, and found that peace to be intolerable. Given the lack of comprehension of Japan's values and will in Washington, a reliable, predictable, and effective U.S. deterrence policy was very unlikely.

The Japanese attack and Saddam Hussein's statements quoted above appear to confirm Donald Kagan's finding that challengers' actions can be shaped by pursuit of intangibles: "greater prestige, respect, and deference, in short, honor."[82] The priority Saddam placed on "pride" and the role of honor in Japanese culture appear not to have been well appreciated by U.S. leaders. That the Japanese emphasis on honor could have affected decision-making and led to behavior "beyond the pale" by U.S. standards is suggested by Japanese War Minister General Korechiki Anami's effort to persuade the Japanese Supreme Council to continue the war, even after the U.S. dropping of the atomic bomb. General Anami "called for one last great battle on Japanese soil—as demanded by the national honor, as demanded by the honor of the living and the dead." He argued, "Would it not be wondrous for this whole nation to be destroyed like a beautiful flower?"[83]

Miscalculation of will prior to the attack on Pearl Harbor was a two-way street: U.S. leaders miscalculated Japan's likely response to their threats, and the Japanese rationale for launching the attack on Pearl Harbor was predicated on a miscalculation concerning the U.S. will to fight a protracted war. The Japanese strategy hinged on a fundamental misperception of the United States: that the American public would lose its will to prosecute a war and would thereby provide Japan with an opportunity to reach a negotiated settlement with the United States in Southeast Asia.[84] In contrast to Japanese expectations, the attack on Pearl Harbor generated sustained popular support for the U.S. war effort and closed any hope of conducting a short, limited war. The Japanese

---

82. Kagan, *On the Origins of War*, 569.

83. Quoted in David McCullough, *Truman* (New York: Simon and Schuster, 1992), 459.

84. See Scott Sagan, "Origins of the Pacific War," *Journal of Interdisciplinary History* 18, no. 4 (spring 1988): 914–17.

misassessment of the American will was a fatal miscalculation that transformed a desperate and high-risk gamble into a disaster.

The Iraqi miscalculation in 1990 leading to the invasion of Kuwait appears to have been somewhat similar to that of the Japanese in 1941. Tariq Aziz has spoken of the Iraqi belief that the United States was conspiring with Kuwait to bring Iraq to economic ruin: "We started to realize that there is a conspiracy against Iraq, a deliberate conspiracy against Iraq by Kuwait, organized, [and] devised by the United States." As a result, according to Aziz, "Iraq had no choice but to act, either to be destroyed, to be suffocated and strangled inside its territory or attack the enemy on the outside."[85]

The dynamic that accounts for a highly motivated challenge may easily go unrecognized by a deterrer who ignorantly assumes a generically rational and sensible foe—a challenger who would prefer conciliation to risking the execution of the deterrer's threat. Yet, as the Japanese in 1941 and Iraq in 1990 appear to illustrate, challengers who find the existing course intolerable will be very hard to deter because they are willing to run great risks. When that dynamic involves domestic political considerations, it may be particularly obscure to the deterrer and thus may undermine the likelihood of an effective policy of deterrence.

German-Russian relations in 1914 also illustrate this difficulty. In 1914 Tsar Nicholas II was in a near-desperate domestic political situation: the Russian Empire had lost stature following its defeat in the Russo-Japanese War and was shaken internally by a revolutionary tide, with the result that the position of the tsar and the government was not strong. This weakness became a key variable in the emerging summer crisis of 1914 because one of the tsar's critical claims to political legitimacy was his role as defender of Slavs and Orthodoxy.[86] Had he chosen not to support Orthodox

---

85. Statements by Tariq Aziz, *Frontline*, "The Gulf War, Part I," transcript, 1–2.

86. As observed by Prince Lichnowsky, "The world of Slav orthodoxy had grown accustomed to regard the Czar as its Protector and Supreme Head, not only in political and intellectual but also to some extent in ecclesiastic affairs. This mission, generally known as the Protectorship of Orthodoxy, 'has become indissolubly associated with the crown of the Autocrat of all the Russians,' says Prince Trubetzkoi. . . . The position of the Tsar in the eyes of his own people rests to some extent on the mystic nimbus which surrounds the Russian crown by virtue of its function as the Protector of Orthodoxy and Slavdom, and it is clear that the Tsar could not renounce this mission without forfeiting much of his prestige and,

Serbia in its confrontation with Austria-Hungary, the tsar would have relinquished this important element of his legitimacy, further weakening his authority and power. He saw no recourse but to exercise his ancient duty as protector of the Orthodox Slavs in the Balkans, that is, Serbia.

Germany, for its part, was unaware of this dynamic at work in Russian decision-making and believed Russia to be ill-prepared and unwilling to engage Germany at that time—again, the hope being for a localized conflict. The kaiser also appears to have believed that the tsar would not come to the aid of regicide and support "the assassins of royalty."[87] Although the German minister in Saint Petersburg, Count Friedrich von Pourtales, was made keenly aware of Russia's intentions to support Serbia, he did not report this to Berlin for fear of challenging Berlin's favored assumption of a localized conflict.[88]

We have seen examples of how unrecognized motivation and ignorance can combine to produce unpredictable behavior and conflict not particularly desired by either party. A challenger's misunderstanding and ignorance of the deterrer can lead the challenger to underestimate the credibility of a deterrence commitment and the actual readiness of the deterrer to enforce its commitment. This can lead to behavior by the challenger that is unexpected by the deterrer and the failure of deterrence. As discussed above, this appears to have been at least part of the dynamic behind the Iraqi invasion of Kuwait.

German-British relations in 1939 also appear to reflect such a dynamic.[89] As a result of a lack of military preparedness and the assumption that Hitler, ultimately, would prove reasonable in avoiding another general European war, Neville Chamberlain hoped to moderate Hitler through a policy of appeasement. Yet this policy, obvious since 1937, and the apparent lack of Allied

perhaps, even endangering his throne." Karl Max Lichnowsky, "Delusions (Notes Made in 1915)," in *Heading for the Abyss: Reminiscences by Prince Lichnowsky* (New York: Payson and Clarke, 1928), 21.

87. Stoessinger, *Why Nations Go to War*, 3.

88. See the excellent discussions in Lebow, *Between Peace and War*, 127–29; and Karsten, Howell, and Allen, *Military Threats*, 71–72, 114.

89. See the review of this case in Craig and George, *Force and Statecraft*, 184–93.

determination, led Hitler to discount the British and French commitment to Poland issued on 31 March 1939. As Craig and George note, the Allied commitment suffered from "a confusion of commitment and national interest. Hitler rationalized that Poland was of little value to the Allies and that in the end they would abandon it, like Czechoslovakia."[90]

Because of Chamberlain's policy of appeasement— built on his initial miscalculation of Hitler as generically sensible—Hitler mistook the Allied commitment to Poland as feckless. And with the 23 August 1939 signing of the Molotov-Ribbentrop pact, Hitler considered Poland free for the taking, striking on 1 September with the simple order to his forces to "show no mercy." In the context of Hitler's understandable—but by now mistaken— doubts concerning Allied will and his pact with the Soviet Union, the Allied commitment to Poland and the British resumption of conscription in August simply could not deter the German invasion of Poland.

More than four decades later, Britain faced a similar situation wherein the credibility of its commitment was miscalculated by a challenger, leading that challenger toward an ill-fated path of aggression that surprised the British. Decisions leading to the 1982 Falklands war with Argentina appear to have been affected by a series of reasonable miscalculations. There is little doubt that the desperate political weakness of the junta ruling Argentina led it to view the dispute with Britain over the Falklands as a vehicle for demonstrating its competence—exploiting nationalistic sentiment on the issue and elevating its domestic political authority. As one assessment of the war notes: "Within Argentina, recovery of the 'Malvinas' would not stifle internal dissent, but at least it would unite the nation for a time. It would serve as a vindication of military rule and cleanse the reputation of the armed forces."[91]

Yet the prospect for Argentina's aggression was heightened by the junta's mistaken view that the British commitment to the Falklands was very soft. There appears to have been a dangerous

---

90. Ibid, 191–92.

91. See Max Hasting and Simon Jenkins, *The Battle for the Falklands* (New York: Norton, 1983), 48. This "domestic politics" thesis also is presented in Watman and Wilkening, *U.S. Regional Deterrence Strategies*, 38–40.

combination of a strongly felt need by the junta to act and little appreciation of the possible cost. The Argentine leadership did not regard the seizure of the Falkland Islands as particularly risky. Following the war, General Leopoldo Galtieri, head of the junta, was asked, "Didn't Argentina see the likelihood of the British responding to the invasion as they did?" Galtieri responded that he had assumed some possibility of a strong British reaction, but he had judged the probability of such to be very low: "Though an English reaction was considered a possibility, we did not see it as a probability. Personally, I judged it scarcely possible and totally improbable. In any case, I never expected such a disproportionate answer. Why should a country situated in the heart of Europe care so much for some islands located far away in the Atlantic Ocean; in addition, islands which do not serve any national interest? It seems so senseless to me."[92]

Galtieri's reference to Britain as "a country situated in the heart of Europe" does not reflect a tremendous familiarity with things British. Yet, General Galtieri could join many other leaders, including Chamberlain in 1939, Acheson in 1941, and senior Bush administration officials in 1990, in decrying the senselessness of the opponent's behavior.[93] This demonstrates well the importance of the fact for deterrence policies that what is "sensible" is in the eye of the beholder, and that differing interpretations of sensible behavior can facilitate miscalculations that lead to the failure of deterrence policies.

Great Britain also miscalculated and contributed to the junta's underestimation of British motivation. Britain did not make clear to Argentina the degree of its commitment to the Falklands. For many years the British had been rather reserved about the islands, had downplayed ties to them, and had stalled negotiations with Argentina on the subject. Indeed, as the crisis began to simmer, the British Foreign Office sought to downplay the whole matter as a way of avoiding provocation. This British reaction appears to

---

92. Oriana Fallaci, "Galtieri: No Regrets, No Going Back," *Times* (London), 12 June 1982, 4.

93. The junta also appears to have miscalculated the likely U.S. response to its occupation of the Falklands. It presumed that the United States would remain neutral and hoped that it would dissuade the British from any use of force. See, ibid, 4; and Alexander Haig, *Caveat* (New York: Macmillan, 1984), 291.

have reinforced the junta's doubts concerning the British commitment.

History and Deterrence Policy

In sum, as the above brief descriptions illustrate, leaders do make decisions based on calculations that are outside the boundaries of deterrence theory, not only, or even primarily, because they are limited by psychopathy. Rather, leaders make decisions based on ignorance, misperception, and a misunderstanding of their opponent's values and likely behavior. As Robert O'Neill has observed, "many of those who initiate wars either do not understand what they are doing or fail to realize the size of the gamble they are taking."[94]

Challengers are driven by factors unrecognized by the deterrer, including domestic political exigencies that render them very highly motivated to change the status quo or the anticipated direction of events. Skepticism of a deterrer's commitment has undermined threats that "should" have been regarded as highly credible. And deterrers, anticipating a sensible opponent, frequently have been surprised at how differently an ostensibly rational opponent defines "sensible" behavior. John Stoessinger's conclusion following his assessment of the causes of war in seven case studies is important when thinking about deterrence: "The case material reveals that perhaps the most important single participating factor in the outbreak of war is misperception. Such distortion may manifest itself in four different ways: in a leader's image of himself; a leader's view of his adversary's character; a leader's view of his adversary's intentions toward himself; and finally, a leader's view of his adversary's capabilities and power."[95]

In addition, when challengers are motivated not by tangible goals obvious to the deterrer but by pursuit of "prestige, respect, and deference, in short honor," as Donald Kagan suggests, their

---

94. "The Use of Military Force: Constant Factors and New Trends," *The Changing Strategic Landscape*, part 2, in Adelphi Papers, no. 236 (London: International Institute for Strategic Studies, 1989): 3.

95. Stoessinger, *Why Nations Go to War*, 214.

behavior may easily be unpredictable because the deterrer will be hard-pressed to understand how the challenger defines those qualities and how such a motivation will affect its decision-making. Deterrers, operating with incomplete knowledge and simplified images of the opponent are unlikely to know when and where their deterrence policies will function as desired, as the Gulf war demonstrated.

Each of the factors discussed above can and has led to decision-making outside the informed, rational boundaries specified by deterrence theory, and attempts at deterrence appear to have failed as a result. Deterrence policies cannot succeed by design when basic ingredients as defined in deterrence theory are missing. In the context of such real-world considerations, the presence of nuclear weapons may strengthen a deterrence policy under some circumstances, as may have been the case with Saddam Hussein in 1991. Even the careful manipulation of nuclear threats, however, cannot "ensure" deterrence policies against the possibility of misperception when the deterrer's policy is poorly informed, when the contestants are operating outside the deterrence theory assumption of well-informed rationality, or when the challenger is simply so highly motivated that it will rationally and knowingly accept tremendous risks in pursuit of its goal.

This discussion arrives at the same destination as have virtually all empirical assessments of deterrence: understanding the opponent, its values, motivation, and determination, is critical to the success or failure of deterrence policies. Unless one is very lucky, in the absence of such an understanding, policies of deterrence sooner or later will fail. As the United States ponders policies of deterrence for the second nuclear age, the first positive step will be shedding the overconfident and naive belief that "how to deter" can be known in practice with a high level of certainty, and that deterrence policies backed by nuclear threats will work in the future just as predictably and reliably as they are thought to have worked throughout the Cold War.

Rather, we should recognize that deterrence can fail, even when it "should" hold, and that in prospective WMD crises of the second nuclear age we may not have any confident basis for anticipating whether deterrence will, in fact, fail or hold. Such a perspective would be very different from the accepted Cold War wisdom about deterrence. Yet, whether the U.S. deterrence policy functions as hoped may be determined by many factors, including how that policy is understood and assessed by the opponent, the character of the opponent's decision-making process, its determination, its propensity for risk-taking over the issues in question, and the personality of the opposing leadership.[96] Of the various factors that determine the success or failure of a deterrent threat, the United States will have the capacity through its declarations and actions to shape how the credibility of its commitments *should* be judged by an opponent, but will have little or no influence over many other important factors. To a considerable extent, the effectiveness of U.S. policies of deterrence is "in the hands" of the opponent and outside the U.S. capacity to control or even influence. In addition, in the second nuclear age we are likely to find the elaboration of reliable and effective deterrence policies more difficult than in the past because the United States will have a relatively low level of familiarity with a variety of regional opponents, and the credibility of U.S. commitments will suffer when U.S. interests involved in regional disputes are not judged by the opponent as "intrinsic."

Finally, some regional adversaries of the second nuclear age will likely fall into the category of those states continually beset by economic or political instability, as may China and Russia. Some recent empirical analyses of deterrence indicate that such states are more inclined to "believe that very risky international action will avert a domestic crisis"; consequently, they "will be hard to deter from that action." In U.S. relations with these regional adversaries, "deterrence is likely to be difficult, expensive, effortful, and dependent on accurate information about how the adversary evaluates his situation."[97]

These conclusions certainly do not correspond well to claims by Americans still bound to Assured Vulnerability who think that nuclear threats "to erase them," to turn the opponent "into a sea of

---

96. As Stoessinger concludes, "with regard to the problem of the outbreak of war, the case studies indicate the crucial importance of the personalities of leaders." Ibid., 213.

97. Watman and Wilkening, *U.S. Regional Deterrence Strategies*, 54.

radioactive glass" or "a hole in the ocean," will provide the foolproof deterrent effect desired. We will not be able knowingly to orchestrate "conclusive" policies of deterrence via such threats or any other mechanism. And if by design or chance we do establish such an effective policy, we will not enter into a crisis with the knowledge that our policy will be conclusive. Deterrence is not a solo act; it is a dance for two or more, and we neither control our partners nor know all of their steps. Identifying the implications of this assessment for U.S. deterrence policies in the second nuclear age is the goal of the following chapter.

Chapter 5
Reconsidering the Hubris of Past and Present

In light of the certain prospect of retaliation there has been literally no chance at all that any sane political authority, in either the United States or the Soviet Union, would consciously choose to start a nuclear war. This proposition is true for the past, the present and the foreseeable future.

—McGeorge Bundy, *To Cap the Volcano*, October 1969

China has long-range missiles too, but the probability of a U.S. "massive retaliation" deters it—likewise for Russia.

—*Christian Science Monitor*, May 17, 1996

In Chapter 4 I concluded that deterrence policies, although potentially effective, are inherently unreliable because leaders do not consistently behave in the manner posited in deterrence theory. In addition, this problem is not amenable to definitive correction through the introduction of nuclear threats. By posing a fearsome threat, nuclear weapons may enhance the credibility of a deterrence commitment in some cases, as in the apparent deterrence of Iraqi WMD during the Gulf War. Given the variety of ways policies of deterrence can fail, however, to claim that nuclear threats can reliably and predictably ensure the effectiveness of deterrence policies can only be described as hubris. Unfortunately, this assertion remains prevalent among U.S. defense officials and commentators.

Because it is the challenger who ultimately chooses whether to be deterred but who cannot be controlled predictably, no deterrer, including the United States, can establish deterrence policies that it can be confident are "ensured" or "conclusive." Some may think that in making this point I have raised the standard for deterrence effectiveness to a level that should not be expected (that is, reliable and predictable), only then to critique as a straw man the possibility of ever reaching such heights. Recall, however, the repeated, continuing, and definitive assurances about nuclear deterrence by senior U.S. officials and commentators. I have not created or misconstrued the many confident expressions about nuclear deterrence working at rarefied heights of effectiveness. As illustrated in Chapters 3 and 4, such claims are standard fare; they abound in past and current debates about U.S. deterrence policies. Assertions frequently are offered in the absence of contextual information: no problems that are beyond correction are granted; there is no acknowledged possibility for insuperable miscalculation, confusion, mistakes, misperceptions, or a challenger's seemingly senseless behavior to cause deterrence failure. Such views are so misleading as to put the United States on a dangerous and risky trajectory— suggesting safety and license where neither may exist. And because such views are so common—even in senior government circles—illustrating the danger of their trajectory is worthwhile.

Nevertheless, as Sun Tzu noted, deterrence is a potentially very valuable tool of statecraft, reflecting the "acme of skill." It should not be abandoned simply because it cannot be made conclusive. Rather, deterrence policy should be made as effective as possible—with full appreciation of the prospect for its failure. What are the implications for the second nuclear age of the fact that deterrence is inherently unreliable but too important to abandon?

The Humility of Uncertainty

The first implication of the preceding analysis is that we should resist the temptation, encouraged by the legacy of Assured Vulnerability thinking, to assume that conclusive deterrence policies can be established on the basis of severe threats. The Assured Vulnerability paradigm is known, comfortable, and easy: if all that is necessary for U.S. deterrence policy to be "conclusive" is to wield a nuclear threat sufficient to "turn you into a sea of radioactive glass," the problem of "how to deter" severe provocation already is solved. The United States has such a threat. However, once our knowledge of "how to deter" in the second nuclear age is recognized as limited, then the question of interest and importance can be addressed: How might we increase the prospect that our deterrence policies will work predictably and as hoped to prevent WMD use against U.S. forces, allies, and territory?

There may be different requirements for deterring WMD use against these three different types of targets: U.S. forces, allies, and territory, each of which could be considered an intrinsic interest. Nevertheless, if a particular opponent can be subjected to U.S. deterrence pressure, the challenge is to understand how to structure and communicate suitable U.S. threats and thresholds to that opponent credibly so as to be able to deter severe provocations. A deterrence policy intended to prevent WMD use of any variety must communicate to the opponent that WMD use is the extreme provocation that must be avoided. If this is possible, U.S. leaders may be in the position to deter the extreme provocations they specify, whether a rogue state's WMD use, a particular type of WMD use, or some other highly provocative behavior. If it is possible to design a policy for deterring a particular opponent from extreme provocation, defining for that opponent's vivid understanding the extreme provocation that must be avoided is the responsibility of the U.S. leadership. Because it is the unique opponent armed with WMD that must be deterred in a specific context, creative and ad hoc policy formulation may be necessary, as was demonstrated by the Bush administration in its efforts to deter Iraqi WMD use during the Gulf war.

Know Your Opponent

The initial step in identifying how we might be able to increase the reliability of deterrence policy is to harken back to Sun Tzu's fundamental admonition to "know your enemy."[1] The United States must ascertain whether the challenger in question can be subjected to U.S. deterrence threats and, if so, what type of threats, given the challenger's character, motivation, determination, and political context. Beyond guidance at a high level of abstraction (U.S. threats should be credible, threaten what the opponent values, and so forth), answers to these questions cannot be generalized.

---

1. Sun Tzu, *The Art of War*, trans. Samuel Griffith (New York: Oxford Univ. Press, 1963), 84.

Rather, they will be shaped by the unique circumstances, the context, and the stakes involved.

This initial need to identify whether the opponent can be subjected to U.S. deterrent pressure and what threats are most likely to be effective presupposes other required information. For example, U.S. leaders must identify how to communicate to the opposing leadership with the least distortion of the message. The information must convey, at least in general terms, the existence of a deterrence threat, the conditions under which that threat will be withheld or executed (what is acceptable or unacceptable behavior), and the high degree of U.S. commitment involved. This latter information can affect the level of credibility that an opponent attributes to a deterrent threat and, therefore, the effectiveness of the threat. Deterrence policies in the second nuclear age may involve psychological operations vis-à-vis the challenger that are intended to establish a particular set of beliefs by the challenger concerning the U.S. deterrence commitment.

Conveying information may be possible through a mixture of actions and declarations, but the optimal channels are likely to vary with the particular leaders and context. How messages are presented, when, and by whom can shape the opponent's response. For example, in some political cultures, greater significance would likely be placed on a message delivered by a close relative of the U.S. president than if it were delivered by a local U.S. official or even a senior official from Washington. And, as Alexander George has noted, in some cultures leaders respond "very negatively indeed" to direct threats.[2] In short, an initial step in understanding how to deter is to ascertain whether the challenger can be subject to U.S. pressure, if so, what type of pressure, and how to communicate with the leadership in question—with an appreciation of the factors that will shape the challenger's reception of information and subsequent decision-making.

Communication may not need to be precise; in some cases both parties may seek a level of ambiguity in these areas. For example, U.S. leaders may avoid specifying the precise provocation

---

2. Quoted in "Speaking with Alexander George about 'Coercive Diplomacy,'" *United States Institute of Peace Journal* (October 1991): 2. For a useful summary of George's work, see Alexander George, *Forceful Persuasion* (Washington, D.C.: U.S. Institute of Peace, 1991).

that would lead to execution of the deterrent threat, in the hope that the threat will be effective over a wider range of provocations than they would, in fact, wish to specify. Ambiguity may be useful: NATO's Flexible Response and U.S. declarations about "launch [of ICBMs] under attack" included some intended ambiguity because it was thought to enhance the deterrent effect. A common refrain in U.S. discussions is that such ambiguity is useful for deterrence. It should be recognized, however, that ambiguity may also have the unhelpful effect of encouraging a risk-prone opponent to see an exploitable softness in commitment. The challenge for the United States, again, is one of information. to discern in which cases ambiguity would be helpful or disadvantageous, depending on the character of the challenger and the context.

For U.S. deterrence policies to "work" by design requires considerable familiarity with the challenger and rationality on the part of a challenger who is not so highly motivated as to be "beyond deterrence" in practice. In short, U.S. leaders will need to know the degree to which any particular challenger and context meet these requirements and how and what to communicate with that particular challenger. Effective deterrence policies will, of course, also require a threat that is sufficiently credible to be decisive in the particular opponent's cost-benefit calculations.

There may be cases in which a challenger is deterred in the absence of informed U.S. policy. A challenger may be deterred, for example, by its own internally generated estimate of the risks involved in provoking the United States, independent of any U.S. deterrence policy. Such occasions, however, represent a challenger's self-deterrence, not the success of U.S. policy, and they cannot serve as the basis for a policy of any reliability or predictability.

As U.S. leaders attempt to establish the basis for deterring a particular opponent, the following checklist includes some of the important information about the challenger that will be useful:[3]

---

3. A version of this checklist was first presented in Keith B. Payne, "Counterproliferation: Deterring Emerging Nuclear Actors?" Presentation to the Strategic Options Assessments Conference, sponsored by the U.S. Strategic Command, 7 July 1993, Dougherty Conference Center, Offutt Air Force Base.

- Do you know whom you are attempting to deter?

- Do you know whether the opponent is capable of rational decision-making under stress?

- Does the leadership you have targeted for deterrence actually control policy decisions and military actions? If so, to what degree?

- Can you understand even approximately the opponent's will or resolve in challenging you? Do you know whether there is sufficient softness in the opponent's determination for a U.S. threat to pose an effective deterrent?

- Are you sufficiently familiar with the opponent's decision-making process to be confident that you know how to affect it?

- Can you approximate/understand the decision-maker's value hierarchy and rationality?

- Do you know the types of threats that would dominate the challenger's decision-making and value hierarchy?

- Do you know the opposing leadership's value "thresholds" sufficiently well to avoid situations in which that leadership is "undeterrable" for all practical purposes, or in which your threats will serve to provoke rather than deter?

- Do you know how to communicate reliably with the opponent?

- Have you identified key cultural/idiosyncratic factors and how to accommodate these in your deterrence policy?

- Do you know the level of *credibility* likely to be ascribed to your threats by the opponent? Do you know what factors determine the level of credibility

of your threat in your opponent's view, and can
you affect that level?

Addressing these questions obviously requires detailed
knowledge of the challenger and the context—knowledge that
may be elusive. Nevertheless, U.S. leaders should resist the easy
assumption of a generically sensible foe. Establishing a U.S. deterrence policy that is informed by the answers to these questions
will represent the tailoring of that policy to the given opponent
and context. Such tailoring will be important to the reliability of a
policy because it is the unique opponent under specific circumstances that must be deterred; the convenient assumptions of a
credible commitment and a generically rational and sensible foe
will not be adequate in the second nuclear age (even assuming
that it was in the Cold War).

It is not possible to establish a generic formula for predictably
deterring a rogue challenger, however fearsome U.S. leaders
consider their threat to be. In attempting to establish policies that
are as reliable as possible, we must avoid likening deterrence
policies to men's socks; one size will not fit all. The differences in
leaderships, decision-making processes, risk tolerances, threat
perceptions, goals, values, and determination, and simply the
potential for idiosyncratic behavior, must limit the reliability of
any generic formula for deterrence. With substantial intelligence
about the particular opponent and context to guide U.S. actions,
however, we should be able to improve the effectiveness and
reliability of deterrence policies. In the absence of the types of
substantive information identified above, there can be little
confident basis for making informed recommendations regarding
the manner in which to deter any particular foe from a specific act.

A recommendation that follows from this requirement for substantial information is clear: profiles of challengers, both for key
individuals and for the systems within which they operate, should
be invaluable in orchestrating deterrence policies. These profiles
should be tailored to the type of information pertinent to the
needs of the deterrer; that is, identifying and weighting the factors
that are inputs to and shapers of a particular challenger's decision-
making. Those factors could be as diverse as the character of an
individual leader, the domestic political and economic conditions,

the religious beliefs of a particular leadership group, or the type of regime.[4]

Clearly, a multidisciplinary approach to such profiles would be necessary; included should be psychologists, cultural anthropologists, historians, political scientists, economists, regional area specialists, and military specialists. The more comprehensive and accurate the characterization of the challenger, the better prepared should U.S. policymakers be to tailor deterrence policy to the opponent and context.

Tailoring deterrence policies according to detailed and multidisciplinary analysis of the opponent may seem to be simply common sense. But the Assured Vulnerability approach largely ignores this common sense. Recall that it focuses almost entirely on the character of a U.S. nuclear threat as the determinant of deterrence effectiveness. The challenger is assumed to be well informed, rational, and sensible, and to attribute sufficient credibility to the U.S. commitment. The critical contextual factors are treated as a given and entirely favorable to our strategic deterrence policies working—and not to require investigation.

Even when assessing the one factor seen as variable—the nuclear threat—there was no apparent effort under Minimum Deterrence or MAD to tailor the specific type of threat according to an appreciation of the Soviet Union's values.[5] Fred Kaplan, for example, describes McNamara's formula for assured destruction: "It all appeared scientific and precise, but in fact it had little to do with any formulation of how much would be enough to deter the Soviets. It was the output of a computer program designed by Alain Enthoven 'laying down' 1-megaton bombs against Soviet cities and calculating, at various points, how much additional damage one additional bomb would do."[6]

4. The possible political difficulties involved for those generating such reports were illustrated by the Central Intelligence Agency's unflattering profile of Haitian President Aristide, portions of which became public through congressional briefings at a time of great political inconvenience to the White House. See R. Jeffrey Smith, "CIA Profile of Aristide Debated: GOP Lawmakers Accuse Christopher of Trying to Gloss over Report," *Washington Post*, 5 November 1993, A34.

5. Although, as noted in Chapter 3, "War-Fighting" was at least presented by senior U.S. officials as an effort to tailor the threat to those targets of highest value to the Soviet regime.

6. Fred Kaplan, *The Wizards of Armageddon* (Stanford: Stanford Univ. Press, 1983), 317.

In the second nuclear age, it should be recognized that contextual factors will shape the effectiveness and reliability of U.S. deterrence policies. Intelligence about the challenger and context will be at least as important a contribution to establishing tailored deterrence policies as is the character of the U.S. military threat. Indeed, knowing the opponent in detail must become the first step in identifying "how to deter." Intelligence considerations should take initial precedence over the usual focus on military capability because the character of the U.S. threat should be determined by what is known about the challenger's values and motivations.

Capabilities and Threats

In the second nuclear age, U.S. deterrence policies must be ready to address a wide range of threats. Defense planners concerned about deterrence can no longer afford the luxury of concentrating primarily on one enemy. The U.S. military capabilities suited to deterring across a wide spectrum of challengers may be quite varied with regard to both the type of force-use threatened and the targets selected. This will be the case because of the likely differences in the context involved, opponents' goals and intentions, their respective assessments of utility and their estimates of U.S. credibility, and because different opponents will have different incentives driving their prospective provocation of the United States. The U.S. deterrent threat must be sufficiently flexible to speak to all of these particular opponents and incentives. In some cases, a conventional threat may be suitable; in others, deterrence may require a proportional nuclear, chemical, or biological threat; in still others, a grossly disproportional threat may be needed. Whether effective threats can be implicit and tied to a general identification of actions the challenger must avoid, or must be explicit and tied to precise instructions is, again, likely to depend on the contextual details. In the Gulf war, general expressions of U.S. concern appear to have been insufficient to prevent the invasion of Kuwait. In contrast, the apparently successful deterrence of Iraqi WMD use appears to have been an effect of near-explicit nuclear threats and precise identification of the provocation that Saddam Hussein had to avoid.

The now-common suggestions that U.S. conventional threats will be adequate for deterrence because they increasingly can inflict WMD-type levels of damage, or, in contrast, that nuclear threats will assuredly be necessary because of their lethality, assume a similarity among potential opponents and contexts that almost certainly will not exist. U.S. threats will carry different weights and inspire different types of responses from different leaders in varying contexts. Consequently, the United States may have to draw from a very wide spectrum of capabilities to provide the particular type of threat suited to a particular opponent. To the extent that the United States has at its disposal a wide spectrum of military options from which to choose, the probability is increased that it will have at its disposal the threat suited to the challenger.

It does not necessarily follow, however, that policies of deterrence should be dismissed when the necessary intelligence base is unavailable or ambiguous. Rather, U.S. efforts to deter in such cases should be extended in the full understanding that they may not work; the appropriate U.S. policy should hedge against the possibility of its own failure. When there is insufficient information about the challenger upon which to tailor a specific U.S. deterrent threat, deterrence by "denial" (involving U.S. military threats to the opponent's military capabilities and objectives) as opposed to deterrence by threat of "punishment" (usually thought of as threatening urban/industrial targets à la Minimum Deterrence and MAD)[7] *may* provide an adequate basis for deterrence. More important in this case, however, a denial deterrent could serve as a useful hedge in the event deterrence fails. It could serve a useful purpose, including the physical destruction of the challenger's military capabilities and frustration of the challenger's military goals, thus physically addressing what deterrence was intended to prevent. In short, in the absence of better guidance, deterrence by denial will likely be the prudent approach, providing both the possibility of deterrence and a hedge against its failure.

---

7. For an early presentation of this distinction between deterrence by denial versus deterrence by punishment, see Glen Snyder, *Deterrence and Defense: Toward a Theory of National Security* (Princeton: Princeton Univ. Press, 1961), 15.

Some empirical studies suggest that U.S. regional deterrence policies in the second nuclear age will, in general, be better served by denial threats because of the types of regimes likely to be involved in the challenge.[8] The analysis of regional deterrence by Watman and Wilkening, for example, leads them to conclude that the type of severe nuclear threats to Soviet society that dominated U.S. Cold War deterrence declarations may be inappropriate for regional deterrence because "for many Third World regimes, there may be little analogous sense of responsibility or duty toward the population and its welfare. At best, the population and civilian economy are instrumental goods for such regimes. They are valued and protected only insofar as they are important to accomplishing the goals of the regime or individual leaders. More often, the population and civilian economy are viewed with suspicion , a necessary evil unavoidable in the process of holding national power."[9] While holding up Soviet Cold War leaders as benign and caring seems quite a stretch, there obviously are cases, such as with Saddam Hussein or the regime in Pyongyang, where a rogue's instrumental view of its general population would likely affect any cost-benefit calculations and related decision-making. That is, a threat of even massive societal damage may not be an effective basis for deterrence for such a leadership. Punitive deterrence threats may not only be ill-suited for determining the challenger's decision-making in these cases; their actual execution following the failure of deterrence would likely serve little or no immediately useful purpose.

As the United States continues to move its nuclear forces to the "background" and to draw down U.S. conventional forces deployed abroad, it must be prepared to construct deterrence policies that are less reliant on conventional or nuclear forces stationed overseas. Because U.S. forward-based conventional and nuclear forces are rapidly being withdrawn, and because U.S. strategic nuclear threats are likely to be judged by U.S. officials as inappropriate for regional deterrence in many possible cases (discussed below), U.S. regional deterrence policies may have to

---

8. Kenneth Watman and Dean Wilkening, *U.S. Regional Deterrence Strategies* (Santa Monica, Calif.: RAND 1995), 54.

9. Ibid., 4–5.

be built largely on the threats that can be posed by U.S. force projection capabilities. Again, unless a challenger's profile suggests otherwise, deterrence may be established on a regional rogue's fear that its aggression could lead to a rapid response by U.S. and allied expeditionary forces capable of defeating its military and frustrating its objectives—once again, deterrence by denial. The U.S. capability to project force and frustrate an aggressor's theory of military victory in a region could make regional aggression by local bullies an unattractive option. In this case, the threat upon which deterrence policies could be built would involve the same forces that would be employed in the event deterrence failed: U.S. expeditionary forces for regional war-fighting.

Compared to its role in containing the Soviet Union during the Cold War, force projection—the ability to send expeditionary forces overseas and sustain them in temporary peacetime deployments or combat operations—may have to sustain the primary burden for deterring future regional challenges to the United States, its interests, and its allies.[10] The United States will retain worldwide security commitments, even as it reduces and withdraws forces that support those obligations. The Army, Navy, Air Force, and Marine Corps all will be considerably smaller. For political as well as fiscal reasons, fewer troops, tanks, ships, and aircraft will be permanently stationed abroad.

While portions of the post–Cold War force can be used to maintain a forward presence in Southwest Asia, Northeast Asia, and Europe, the United States cannot concentrate its military power in any single region. U.S. interests are global, potential adversaries are diverse, possible conflict areas are scattered, the time and place of aggression are difficult to forecast, and U.S. forces are limited. Expeditionary forces that can reach far-off allies and war zones in a timely manner from bases in the United States will be needed to meet this approach to deterrence policy in the second nuclear age. Whereas U.S. forces deployed abroad provide forward presence, quick-reaction expeditionary forces offer a "distant presence" that may also reassure friends and discourage

---

10. This section draws heavily on an unpublished report by Kurt Guthe and Keith Payne, *Deterrence, Power Projection, and Long-Range Airpower* (Fairfax, Va.: National Security Research, 1993), pp. 7-13.

enemies. In short, the force projection capabilities of a smaller, less far-flung U.S. military may help bridge the gap between strategic ends and the military means available to support deterrence policies.

To support regional deterrence policies and a capability for fighting regional opponents, what attributes should such U.S. expeditionary forces ideally possess? In addition to having global reach, these forces should be flexible, rapid, autonomous, powerful (even awe-inspiring), and low-risk. Flexibility is valuable because forces that are highly specialized to deal with a particular enemy, type of conflict, or opposing force may be limited in their utility, costly to retain, and insufficiently adaptable to political and military-technical change. Given at best flat defense budgets, shrinking force structure, and uncertainties about the location and character of future challengers, forces that are suitable for a wide range of contingencies and a variety of purposes are preferrable. Moreover, flexible forces are more readily integrated in combined-arms packages tailored to specific sets of political-military circumstances.

Expeditionary forces that can deploy rapidly to foreign locations have a number of advantages. The manifest ability of U.S. forces to help in defending an allied country within days or possibly hours of an enemy provocation or attack may contribute to the credibility of distant presence and U.S. security commitments. At the same time, challengers may find the prospect of swift U.S. counteraction more daunting, and thus deterring, than a slow response. Speed can diminish the military effects of a surprise attack against a U.S. ally or, as is often the case, the failure to react to ambiguous warning of an attack. Similarly, fast-moving forces can offset some of the adverse consequences of delays in mobilization and deployment potentially caused by prolonged political deliberations in Washington and allied capitals (including negotiations over U.S. access to foreign bases). In the case of a major enemy offensive against a friendly country, the manifest capability for a rapid counterattack may be necessary to prevent a challenger from anticipating irreversible gains: seizure of vital territory, destruction of ports and airfields otherwise available for U.S. forces, even the surrender of the allied government. Such an anticipation could increase the benefit side of a challenger's cost-benefit calculations to the detriment of U.S. deterrence policy. In some conflicts, failure to halt a ground attack quickly could increase by two or three times the number of divisions needed for a later counteroffensive. By the same token, expected U.S. casualties would increase,[11] possibly fueling expectations that U.S. political leaders would decide against intervention, and the potential that a regional rogue could conceive of a theory of victory.

Ideally, the effective threat of U.S. force projection should not be dependent on substantial support from other force elements or the presence of well-prepared, in-theater bases. This would be especially true in the initial stages of a large-scale U.S. military intervention. Pending future improvements, capabilities for rapid airlift and sealift of men and materiel are likely to be overtaxed for one, let alone two major regional conflicts. Support elements may be inherently less flexible, rapid, and autonomous than the projection forces they assist. Bases in or near the theater of operations may be nonexistent or inadequate. In some cases, access to usable bases may be denied by the governments that control them, perhaps because of intimidation by the aggressor. While proximity to the war zone will make the support of combat operations easier, it also may make forward bases vulnerable to air or missile attacks. Expeditionary forces able to operate from more remote and austere bases could deploy to a wider range of locations for any given contingency.

Expeditionary capabilities for deterrence purposes should be powerful in the estimate of the challenger. Token force deployments, such as lightly armed airborne troops positioned to block large, heavy armor formations, may be insufficient for deterrence, and certainly for defense against a well-armed adversary. Once considered "tripwires" (that when attacked would elicit a major military response by the United States), they now are more like hostages that if threatened could prompt a U.S. military withdrawal—possibly contributing to challengers' doubts of U.S. credibility. Heavy, mobile, and focused firepower, rather than to-

---

11. Secretary of Defense Les Aspin, *Force Structure Excerpts: Bottom-Up Review*, 1 September 1993, 7 (mimeographed); Secretary of Defense Les Aspin, remarks at the National Defense University Graduation, 16 June 1993, 2 (mimeographed).

ken forces, might be necessary for the expectation of military effect that would shape a challenger's decision-making.

Such capabilities could, in particular, deny regional challengers the anticipation of achieving a *fait accompli* vis-à-vis the United States.[12] This may be particularly important because, according to some empirical analyses of deterrence, challengers' anticipation of a *fait accompli* is one of the primary dynamics behind the failure of deterrence policies.[13]

The U.S. capability for rapid and decisive force projection could also help dispel a challenger's expectation that it might exploit a widely perceived U.S. political weakness: the widespread view of unwillingness on the part of the American public and the Congress to support prolonged military intervention and accept high levels of casualties.[14] Recall that the expectation of this U.S. political vulnerability helped move the Japanese in 1941 and Saddam Hussein in 1990 toward provocation. While different polling evidence can be interpreted as validating or contesting the accuracy of this widespread perception of U.S. political vulnerability,[15] challengers' expectation of its effect on U.S. decision-making undoubtedly has been a past trigger for provocation of the United States, and consequently it has been a dynamic for the failure of the U.S. capacity to deter and coerce. The manifest U.S. capability to project forces swiftly and decisively could help dispel the notion that this is an exploitable vulnerability.

---

12. Interestingly, a recent North Korean commentary on Pyongyang's strategy for deterring U.S. support to South Korea in the event of conflict focuses on presenting the U.S. with a military fait accompli, and then deterring further U.S. involvement with missile and WMD threats. See Kim Myong Chol, "North Korea Prepared to Fight to the End as Kim Jong-il Has His Own Version of *The Art of War*," *Asia Times*, 10 April 1996, 9.

13. As discussed in Paul Huth, *Extended Deterrence and the Prevention of War* (New Haven: Yale Univ. Press, 1988), 86.

14. As Watman and Wilkening observe in this regard: "One of the more troubling reputations the United States has acquired is for heightened sensitivity to casualties. Many foreign, as well as American , leaders believe that U.S. public opinion will turn against any conflict or war as soon as U.S. casualties begin to mount, leading the public to demand withdrawal. This sensitivity implies that U.S. threats to intervene are less credible." Watman and Wilkening, *U.S. Regional Deterrence Strategies*, 59. This expected U.S. lack of political will is a primary factor behind the argument for a very selective U.S. approach to any expeditionary undertaking. See Jonathan Clarke and James Clade, *After the Crusade* (Lanham, Md.: Madison Books, 1995), 65–84.

15. See, Watman and Wilkening, *U.S. Regional Deterrence Strategies*, 59. See also Guthe and Payne, *Deterrence, Power Projection*, 11–12.

In short, to help move potential challengers away from anticipating that their provocation of the United States could go unanswered, or insufficiently answered for deterrence purposes, the capability for rapid and decisive force projection could be a key to U.S. deterrence policies in the second nuclear age.

A Deterrence Role for Nuclear Weapons

Some analyses of regional deterrence indicate that conventional threats may be inadequate because a challenger may believe it can withstand even "the most devastating conventional punishment" for an extended period.[16] This certainly appears to have been a dynamic behind Iraqi thinking before the Gulf war. When Secretary of State James Baker told Iraqi Foreign Minister Tariq Aziz of the "overwhelming" conventional power that would be "brought to bear" against Iraq, Aziz responded, "Mr. Secretary, Iraq is a very ancient nation. We have lived for 6000 years. I have no doubts that you are a very powerful nation. I have no doubts that you have a very strong military machine and you will inflict on us heavy losses. But Iraq will survive and this leadership will decide the future of Iraq."[17] In contrast, implicit U.S. *nuclear* threats appear to have had the desired deterrent effect.

In some cases, nuclear weapons may thus be a key to deterrence policy success: the sheer fearsomeness of nuclear weapons, if appreciated by the challenger, may be a critical component for effective deterrence. This is not to suggest that U.S. deterrence policy can be "ensured" via nuclear threats; it cannot. However, in those cases where the contextual conditions necessary for deterrence are present and the challenger is risk- and cost-tolerant—but nevertheless maleable by severe threat—nuclear weapons may be decisive in the challenger's decision-making when conventional threats would not be. Such occasions may admittedly be infre-

---

16. George Quester and Victor Utgoff, *A Discussion of Internationalizing Nuclear Security Policy*, Project on Rethinking Arms Control, Paper no. 15 (College Park: Center for International and Security Studies at Maryland, 1995), 1.

17. Statements by James Baker and Tariq Aziz, *Frontline*, "The Gulf War, Part I," no. 1407, 9 January 1996, transcript, 9.

quent. But for deterrence to work on those occasions could be of tremendous value.

In addition, nuclear deterrence threats may be important in regional contingencies where the U.S. commitment is not recognized by the challenger as "intrinsic." As noted above, some empirical analyses of deterrence indicate that "fearsome" military capabilities can, to some extent, compensate for questions about a deterrer's resolve to enforce its threat.[18] The capacity of nuclear threats to compensate for doubts about U.S. determination may help explain why Saddam Hussein, who was very dubious of U.S. resolve, nevertheless was deterred from WMD use during Desert Storm.

In short, the presence of nuclear weapons as a key element in U.S. deterrence policy may contribute to preventing self-serving conclusions by challengers concerning the ultimate costs of provoking the United States. Nuclear weapons cannot render deterrence reliable with any certainty, although such is frequently asserted by senior U.S. officials. In some cases, however, they may help impress otherwise hardened challengers with the extreme risks involved in extreme provocations.

The potential need for U.S. nuclear threats to backstop regional deterrence policies is in some conflict with the obvious drive to move U.S. nuclear weapons increasingly to the "background"[19] as part of a general goal to strengthen the taboo against use of nuclear weapons.[20] This taboo is consistent with the view generally held by U.S. political leaders that the use of nuclear weapons, virtually by definition, is disproportionate to U.S. goals

---

18.   Watman and Wilkening, *U.S. Regional Deterrence Strategies*, 57.

19.   That nuclear weapons are intended to play a reduced role is presented officially in William Perry, *Annual Report to the President and the Congress* (Washington, D.C.: GPO, March 1996), 15; and, Perry, *Annual Report to the President and the Congress* (Washington, D.C.: GPO, February 1995), 83. The goal of moving nuclear weapons to the "background," and specifically the view that the use of nuclear weapons could be legitimate only in response to a challenger's prior first-use, is developed in a 1992 book whose co-authors include the current secretary of defense and assistant secretary of defense for international security policy. See Ashton Carter, William Perry, and John Steinbruner, *A New Concept of Cooperative Security* (Washington, D.C.: Brookings Institution, 1992), 11–12.

20.   Perry, Carter, and Steinbruner, for example, argued in 1992 that with the ending of the East-West confrontation "at hand . . . is the prospect for a radical deemphasis of nuclear weapons in the security conceptions of the major powers." The goal of this "radical deemphasis" in large measure is "toward inducing others to deemphasize them." Ibid., 12–13.

in a regional crisis. This American perspective is well recognized internationally, potentially reducing the credibility of regional U.S. deterrence threats.

Indeed, the United States has sought to strengthen the nuclear taboo in regional considerations. For example, as part of a package of "negative security assurances" the United States formally has pledged as policy not to use nuclear weapons against non-nuclear states that are party to the Non-Proliferation Treaty or any comparable internationally binding commitment not to acquire nuclear devices, except in the case of attack by a signatory allied or associated with a nuclear weapons state. This U.S. pledge of nonuse was announced by Secretary of State Cyrus Vance in 1978 and has been reaffirmed by the Clinton administration.[21] In addition, beginning in the early 1990s, the United States began withdrawing most of its theater nuclear weapons, and few remain with U.S. forces abroad.[22] The deterrent value that might be contributed by the fearsome destructive potential of remaining theater and strategic nuclear weapons may be reduced by the widespread perception, encouraged by U.S. declarations and behavior, that their use could not be compatible with any regional U.S. interest.

Following the Gulf war, for example, former President Bush was asked, "Are there any circumstances in which you actually had a nuclear option, or do you think . . . that it would be very difficult for any president to exercise that?" President Bush's response reflects the general and powerful internal taboo against U.S. nuclear use in regional contingencies: "I still stay with that view, that it would be extraordinarily difficult. I suppose you could conjure up some horrible scenario that would call for the

---

21.   See Cyrus Vance's statement presented in U.S. Arms Control and Disarmament Agency, *Arms Control and Disarmament Agreements: Texts and Histories of the Negotiations* (Washington, D.C.: ACDA, 1990), 94. All the five "nuclear weapon states" have some form of declared negative security guarantee for NPT members, but these guarantees are not all the same. See *The Arms Control Reporter 1995* (Cambridge, Mass.: Institute for Defense and Disarmament Studies, 1995), 850.393–850.395.

22.   See U.S. Secretary of Defense Les Aspin, "From Deterrence to Denuking: Dealing with Proliferation in the 1990s," 18 February 1992, 15 (mimeographed). As the Pentagon's 1995 report to Congress states, "In recent years there has been a dramatic reduction in both the overall size of the U.S. military presence abroad and in the nuclear capabilities deployed overseas." Perry, *Annual Report to the President and the Congress* (February 1995), 84.

use of battlefield tactical nuclear weapons or something, but it was not something that we really contemplated at all."[23] In discussing the possibility of U.S. nuclear use at the time General Colin Powell said to Defense Secretary Cheney, "Let's not even think about nukes, you know we're not going to let that genie lose." Cheney replied, "Of course not."[24]

On 3 April 1994, in the context of the crisis with North Korea over its nuclear weapons program, Secretary of Defense Perry provided an equally definitive rejection of nuclear use. When asked on *Meet the Press*, "What about the possibility of the use of nuclear weapons, if it would save American lives?" Secretary Perry replied, "I can't envision the circumstances in which the use of nuclear weapons would be reasonable or prudent military action."[25]

This great reluctance on the part of U.S. political leaders to consider the use of nuclear weapons is neither new nor the result of a lack of military experience. In 1954, President Eisenhower, responding to a National Security Council staff paper concerning the possibility of using low-yield nuclear weapons to relieve the French forces besieged in Dien Bien Phu, said, "You boys must be crazy. We can't use those awful things against Asians for a second time in less than ten years. My God."[26] Clearly, the effect of the nuclear taboo among American leaders had begun by 1954 and may have been a factor in their earlier nonuse by Truman during the Korean War.[27]

This discussion should not necessarily be misunderstood as advocacy of U.S. regional nuclear use, increased nuclear capabilities, or the deployment of U.S. theater nuclear forces. It simply points to the strong feeling among U.S. political leaders that the use of nuclear weapons is disproportionate to regional interests—even long-standing U.S. security commitments.

23.   President Bush, in *A Gulf War Exclusive: President Bush Talking with David Frost*, Transcript no. 51, 16 January 1996, 5.

24.   Colin Powell, *My American Journey* (New York: Random House, 1995), 486.

25.   NBC News, *Meet the Press*, 3 April 1994, transcript, 7–8.

26.   Quoted in Stephen Ambrose, *Eisenhower the President* (New York: Simon and Schuster, 1984), 184.

27.   See the discussion in Carl Kaysen, Robert McNamara, George Rathjens, "Nuclear Weapons after the Cold War," *Foreign Affairs* 70, no. 4 (Fall 1991): 100.

Declarations and behavior that contribute to the general perception of this very strong U.S. reluctance to use nuclear weapons *in extremis* may be disadvantageous for deterrence in the second nuclear age, particularly as the U.S. confronts regional challengers armed with chemical and biological weapons. Fortunately, Saddam Hussein's decision-making appears not to have been shaped by an appreciation of this nuclear taboo held by U.S. leaders; the exploitation of it by a challenger more familiar with the United States political culture may affect a future regional crisis.

Because the United States has eschewed the possession and use of chemical and biological weapons, we will be limited to conventional or nuclear threats in our future deterrence policies. If a regional challenger armed with biological or chemical weapons judges a U.S. conventional threat as insufficient to be decisive in its decision-making,[28] and if it considers the U.S. regional nuclear threat to be incredible—believing the numerous U.S. expressions to that effect—then a reliable U.S. deterrent may not be possible.[29] Clearly there is some friction here between the long-standing taboo against regional nuclear use and the possible U.S. need for credible nuclear threats in support of regional deterrence policies in the second nuclear age.

---

28. Following the initial experiences with chemical weapons in World War I, they were not used in Europe or by the Japanese against the United States in World War II. These and several additional cases of nonuse typically are attributed, at least in part, to defenses and the deterrent threat of retaliation in kind. In several cases of chemical use (for example, Italian use against Ethiopia in 1935, Japanese use against Chinese forces beginning in 1937, and Egyptian use against Yemen in 1967), the target essentially was defenseless and incapable of retaliation in kind. While not conclusive by any means, these cases suggest the possibility that the presence of defenses and the capability for retaliation in kind may contribute to the deterrence of chemical weapon use. See, for example, the discussion in U.S. Army Concepts Analysis Agency, Strategy and Plans Directorate, *Chemical Deterrence (CHEMDET), Phase I—Historical Background*, June 1992.

29. It should be noted that just as this manuscript was going to print Secretary of Defense Perry made an implicit but nonetheless clear effort to inform potential adversaries that they should consider nuclear weapons as part of the U.S. repertoire for responding to the use of WMD against the United States and its allies: "We continue to maintain a nuclear deterrence considerably smaller than during the Cold War, but make no mistake, still absolutely devastating in its destructive power. Anyone who considers using a weapon of mass destruction against the United Sates or its allies must first consider the consequences. ... Our response. .. would be both overwhelming and devastating." It is unclear how this implicit nuclear warning to any challenger considering WMD use can be compatible with the U.S. "negative security assurances" discussed above. See, remarks by Defense Secretary William Perry at Georgetown University, 18 April 1996, Federal News Service, 19 April 1996, 2.

Because forward-deployed nuclear weapons may not be readily available for some regional crises, home-based strategic nuclear
forces may be important for regional deterrence. Those U.S.
strategic delivery systems that appear to be most compatible with
the degree of flexibility and force projection that we may need to
support regional deterrence policies include most prominently
strategic bombers capable of delivering a variety of weapons,
whether nuclear or conventional. Strategic bombers can threaten
to destroy a wide range of targets, including deep underground
facilities, and can deliver with great accuracy one or multiple
weapons of varying yields. The recent apparent U.S. move toward
a minimalist purchase of twenty-one B-2 heavy strategic bombers
may be a mistake in terms of future deterrence needs, as it probably is insufficient to sustain an operational force in support of
multiple regional war-fighting contingencies. Again, this is not to
argue for more strategic nuclear forces overall. Indeed, we may be
able to gain whatever value strategic nuclear forces can contribute
to regional deterrence at much reduced force levels. Those forces
intended for regional deterrence duties, however, should offer the
flexibility needed for a great variety of potential opponents and
circumstances and be compatible with our own values.

The possible role for nuclear weapons in compensating for an
apparent weakness of resolve points to one of the primary problems likely to confront U.S. deterrence policies in the second nuclear age: how to inspire the challenger to attribute resolve to U.S.
deterrence commitments for nonintrinsic interests. Nuclear
weapons may assist in presenting a fearsome threat, but empirical
studies typically point to the requirement for a historical record of
commitment to a state if threats on its behalf are to be judged as
credible by challengers. As Gordon Craig and Alexander George
note in this regard, "Deterrence is not simply a matter of announc-
ing a commitment and backing it with threats. The validity of a
given commitment is directly related to its possessing a demon-
strable or reasonable relationship to the maker's real national interests."[30]

---

30. Craig and George, *Force and Statecraft*, 191. Watman and Wilkening reach this
same conclusion in their empirical analysis of deterrence: "Moreover, commitments cannot
be created at the time of a crisis. Time is needed to develop a network of political,
economic, and military ties with an endangered state. This means that the most credible

It is difficult to anticipate how foes who are poorly informed or apparently lacking sense will grade U.S. commitments and the credibility of U.S. threats. Challengers who are informed, rational, and sensible, however, should attribute a high level of credibility to U.S. deterrence commitments for those states and geographical areas where the United States has a long historical record of ties and commitment, including North America, much of Latin America, Western Europe, South Korea, Japan, and Israel. To assume that even sensible and informed challengers would give our deterrence efforts high marks for credibility elsewhere on the basis of declarations at the time of an acute crisis is likely to pose a risk. For those areas, nuclear threats may be necessary to compensate; but of course the "catch-22" here is that in those areas where historical ties and commitments are lacking, the U.S. may be recognized by the challenger as least likely to consider nuclear use proportional to any goal.

Our confidence in policies of deterrence in cases where nonintrinsic interests are at stake should not be high, particularly against a highly motivated challenger. We will likely not be able to create "instant" credibility for impromptu commitments in areas of limited U.S. historical involvement. In such areas where we can now anticipate the potential need to deter regional challengers, initiating "show the flag" military activities, such as joint exercises in cooperation with local friends, could help begin to establish the necessary historical record. Such activities would be cost-effective in comparison to discovering that we had to protect an interest or friend because a challenger did not give sufficient weight to our commitment, à la Korea in 1950.

Missile Defense

This assessment of deterrence in the second nuclear age has several important implications for ballistic missile defense (BMD), both theater missile defense (TMD) and national missile defense

---

commitment is one established well before the crisis and continually reinforced by tangible actions. Signals of commitment at the time of crisis may be useful to remind an adversary of an existing commitment, but they cannot establish that commitment in the absence of an historical record." *U.S. Regional Deterrence Strategies*, 62.

(NMD)—the former being defense against short- and medium-range offensive missiles, the latter, defense of the United States against long-range missiles. Given the proliferation of missiles and WMD, both the need to deny regional challengers their deterrent, as discussed in Chapter 2, and the recognition that deterrence policies may fail, suggest important new roles for missile defense. This new importance is in sharp contrast to the view of BMD under Assured Vulnerability, which typically led to an assessment of NMD as being unnecessary and "destabilizing."

For several reasons BMD in the second nuclear age will be viewed more sympathetically, even as essential. First, and most obvious, if deterrence fails or does not apply in a future crisis, BMD, if effective, would provide unique protection for population centers and military forces against WMD-armed ballistic missiles. This "safety net" against deterrence failure would be extremely important in some scenarios, such as when a challenger is armed with a relatively small arsenal of missiles. BMD, in this case, might provide protection for urban areas that otherwise would be vulnerable to devastating WMD-armed missile strikes. It should be noted in this regard that the U.S. and South Korea agreed to the delivery of Patriot missile defenses to Seoul within days of a direct threat from North Korean diplomat Park Young-su: "Seoul is not very far from here. Seoul will turn into a sea of fire."[31] Clearly, if the effectiveness of deterrence is suspect, defensive capabilities necessary to survive its failure are key.

A defensive safety net is particularly important in circumstances in which information about a regional challenger's missile and WMD capability is unclear and in which there is significant uncertainty about how and when WMD might be used against the United States or its allies. For example, recent revelations suggest that even multi-year, highly intrusive UN inspections following the Gulf war were unable to detect large portions of the Iraqi WMD program, including a weaponized biological warfare capability that was deployed in the field at air bases and missile

---

31. Quoted in Ju-Yeon Kim, "N. Korea Tantrum Escalates Anxiety," *Washington Times*, 20 March 1994, 1; and R. Jeffrey Smith, "Clinton Orders Patriot Missiles to South Korea," *Washington Post*, 22 March 1994, 1.

sites during the war.[32] In the context of ambiguity about an opponent's capabilities, intentions, and deterrence effectiveness, missile defenses may provide a level of protection for urban areas that cannot otherwise be achieved.

Missile defense may also provide potentially important political, economic, and military benefits vis-à-vis WMD-armed challengers. The availability of missile defenses may be critical to U.S. and allied decision-making in regional crises where, for example, a challenger's anticipation of U.S. force projection may be necessary for deterrence or for war-fighting following the failure of deterrence. Without relevant defensive capabilities, the risk of significant American and allied casualties resulting from projecting force abroad could be too high for any president to accept. In this environment, missile defense may increase the credibility of the U.S. force projection threat by reducing the challenger's capacity to threaten U.S. expeditionary forces with WMD.

As another example, a challenger's WMD-armed ballistic missiles could threaten a variety of U.S. force projection assets, including ground maneuver forces, aircraft facilities, seaports and harbors, merchant shipping, power and water plants, and fleet operation areas.[33] If rogue challengers judge that because of U.S. missile defense they are less able to threaten such U.S. expeditionary force assets or in the future are less able to threaten U.S. territory, then the deterrent and coercive value of their WMD may be reduced and challengers may be less inclined to provoke U.S. force projection threats. This role for missile defense was illustrated when the U.S. Patriot battalion sent to South Korea in 1994 was positioned for the protection of deployed U.S. forces and the port of Pusan.[34]

The economic impact of "militarily useless" missiles, when used as terror weapons against civilian centers, can be serious. If confidence in deterrence cannot be high, here again is a potentially important need for defense. During the "War of the Cities," for

---

32. R. Jeffrey Smith, "U.N. Says Iraqis Prepared Germ Weapons in Gulf War," *Washington Post*, 26 August 1995, 1.

33. See the discussion in Robert Soofer, "Joint Theater Missile Defense Strategy," *Joint Forces Quarterly*, no. 9 (autumn 1995): 71.

34. Ibid., 72.

example, Iraqi missile attacks essentially shut down the Iranian war economy as workers sought refuge. Israel faced a similar problem during the early days of the Gulf war as civilians frequently were confined to, or close by, their shelters in anticipation of Iraqi Scuds armed with chemical warheads. As Israeli Defense Minister Moshe Arens observed at the time, "As long as the missile threat hangs over Israel, our entire economy is in low gear. We must return to normalcy and put away the gas masks."[35] BMD protection for civilian centers could help address this problem and thereby help preserve U.S. and allied capabilities and resolve to engage regional challengers armed with WMD and missiles.

Although it is far from certain, the presence of missile defenses might contribute to regional stability by offering assurances to parties concerned about surprise attacks. In a regional crisis, the threat posed by an opponent's missiles could encourage preventive or preemptive strikes—which could in turn provoke escalation. In this case, missile defenses could help moderate the incentives for precipitate escalation. In this scenario, active defenses may extend decision-making time and reduce the impact of not preempting early, helping to keep a lid on conflicts.

Similarly, missile defense offers what may be a more desirable alternative to offensive retaliation for cases in which the latter could pose too great a risk. The clearest example involves Israel during the Gulf war. U.S. Patriot batteries, although not wholly effective, provided the "cover" essential to forestalling Israeli reprisals against Iraq, reprisals that likely would have undermined the political cohesion of the Coalition. In this case missile defense provided a level of reassurance to the Israeli population and political leadership that ultimately was important to the outcome of the conflict.

Finally, rather than undermining traditional diplomatic arms control efforts, effective missile defense may contribute to nonproliferation measures. Because missile defense will constitute a unique means of protecting against some of the threats posed by proliferation, it could undermine the military and political value that many regional rogues now attribute to missiles, reducing the

---

35.   Moshe Arens, *Broken Covenant* (New York: Simon and Schuster, 1995), 212.

incentives to acquire, market, or maintain missiles. In this way, missile defenses may help reduce the demand for missiles and complement traditional diplomatic efforts to control the supply side of the missile proliferation equation.

There is some historical precedent for suggesting this positive relationship between missile defense and diplomatic nonproliferation efforts. For example, in the late 1980s a Middle Eastern country proposed to the U.S. that a "missile-free zone" be established in the Middle East, based on cooperation by the potential parties with the United States in the area of missile defense.[36] In 1994 the Russian Federation proposed an international ban on all theater-range missiles, *in the context of cooperation on missile defense.*[37] The rationale for integrating missile defense with diplomatic efforts to limit regional missile arsenals is that missile defenses could reduce the perceived value of offensive missiles, making them easier to give up under such efforts; defenses would provide protection for parties to the agreement against nonsignatories and the possibility of cheating. In short, missile defense could both reduce the incentives to acquire or maintain missiles and help provide the confidence governments would need to participate in a general agreement to give up the missile option.

In short, missile defenses could provide an essential defensive capability should deterrence fail and regional powers resort to the use of WMD and missiles against the United States and/or its allies. In addition, U.S. regional deterrence policies could be strengthened by missile defenses if they helped reduce the capacity of regional challengers to deter and coerce U.S. and allied leaders through WMD threats to power projection forces, urban centers, or both. Missile defense could contribute to deterrence in such cases by helping to protect both the U.S. capability to inter-

---

36. Interview with Dr. Kathleen Bailey, former assistant director for nonproliferation for the Arms Control and Disarmament Agency, interviewed by the author, 7 July 1993.

37. As announced in a presentation by Victor Slipchenko of the Russian Foreign Ministry at Lawrence Livermore National Laboratory, 15 November 1994, Livermore, California. At an off-the-record briefing held in Washington, D.C., a retired senior Indian military officer stated that both India and Pakistan would likely be sympathetic to an agreement to give up ballistic missiles in the context of BMD protection. The retired senior officer indicated that such an arrangement could take several years to establish.

vene and the will to do so. Finally, missile nonproliferation efforts may be advanced as BMD devalues ballistic missiles as delivery vehicles.

National missile defense, which was considered the enemy of deterrence stability and arms control under the Assured Vulnerability paradigm, should be considered much more sympathetically in the second nuclear age. This conclusion was reached by the principal American architect of the 1972 ABM Treaty, a treaty that severely limited NMD in deference to the Cold War concept of deterrence stability:

> The end of the Cold War has made such a strategy [Mutual Assured Destruction] largely irrelevant. Barely plausible when there was only one strategic opponent, the theory makes no sense in a multipolar world of proliferating nuclear powers. Mutual destruction is not likely to work against religious fanatics; desperate leaders may blackmail with nuclear weapons; blackmail or accidents could run out of control. And when these dangers materialize, the refusal to have made timely provision will shake confidence in all institutions of government. At a minimum, the rudiments of a defense system capable of rapid expansion should be put into place.[38]

Moving forward with NMD to protect against future threats by regional challengers need not interfere with the established Assured Vulnerability approach to deterrence with Russia for the foreseeable future. An NMD of modest scope could offer a potentially useful level of protection against regional challengers. Establishing an effective defense against such limited missile threats appears to be possible and affordable. As Defense Secretary Perry recently stated, defense against a rogue attack involving "several dozens of warheads . . . is quite achievable with present technology, and it's achievable with several tens of billions of dollars, not several hundreds of billions of dollars."[39]

---

38. Henry Kissinger, "Ready for Revitalizing," *Los Angeles Times*, 9 March 1995, A21.

39. Remarks by Secretary of Defense William Perry at the Regional Commerce and Growth Association of St. Louis, Missouri, September 28, 1995, Federal News Service, 11–12.

Achieving this capability without undermining a Russian "assured destruction" retaliatory capability also appears to be possible, even at the significantly reduced strategic offensive force levels of START II.[40]

This notion of retaining Assured Vulnerability vis-à-vis the Russian Federation but not permitting U.S. vulnerability to other possible challengers' missiles harkens back to a 1969 proposal by former Defense Secretary Harold Brown. At the time (when the Soviet Union had fewer than 1,800 strategic missile warheads) Brown suggested acquisition of "several hundred" NMD interceptors to deal with "third-country attacks" without upsetting deterrence stability vis-à-vis the Soviet Union.[41] Striking this balance will be even more important in the second nuclear age. We will need to address the threats posed by proliferation while avoiding gratuitous provocation of the Russian Federation. The possible friction involved in moving forward with NMD to help address the emerging proliferation threat already has become apparent: Russia has linked ratification of the START II agreement to strict preservation of the ABM Treaty and its severe limitations on NMD.

This friction, however should be manageable, given even a modicum of U.S.-Russian political cooperation.[42] The key here appears to be whether relatively modest U.S. NMD capabilities can be made effective against third-country threats but kept clearly insufficient against the Russian retaliatory potential.[43]

---

40.   See the pertinent offense-defense computer simulation work by Laura Lee et al., *Assessment of Potential National Missile Defense Capability* (McLean, Va.: Sparta Corp., 1996).

41.   Harold Brown, "Security through Limitations," *Foreign Affairs* 47, no. 3 (April 1969): 430.

42.   Despite the current official hostility toward strategic missile defense coming from Moscow, it should be noted that in January 1992 it was Russian President Boris Yeltsin who proposed U.S.-Russian cooperation on a "Global Protection System" to include missile defense. The Clinton administration did not resume the subsequent talks begun by Presidents Bush and Yeltsin to establish a cooperative "Global Protection System." Nevertheless, there remain supporters of this initiative in Moscow. See, for example, the article by Lt. Gen. Aleksandr Skvortsov, of the Russian General Staff Military Academy, and Maj. Gen. Nikolay Turko, of the Academy of Military Sciences, "Strategic Stability: Key to National Security," *Armeyskiy Sbornik*, no. 1 (January 1996): 4–8. Translated in FBIS-UMA-96-081-S, April 25, 1996, 3.

43.   An ongoing two-year U.S.-Russian study involving prominent U.S. and Russian nongovernmental experts suggests strongly that Russian opposition to U.S.-Russian cooperation on limited NMD can be overcome to the extent that U.S. NMD systems are

Maintaining such a balance in the long run may be difficult if third-country arsenals grow while Russian and U.S. strategic arsenals continue to be reduced through the START process. In the long run, however, officials from both sides have called for moving beyond the old Cold War mutual vulnerability concept as the basis for U.S.-Russian strategic relations.[44]

The goal of "balancing" the continuation of Assured Vulnerability vis-à-vis the Russian Federation with the requirement for protection against rogue missile threats raises an obvious question: If deterrence is inherently unreliable and unpredictable given the variety of mechanisms for its failure, why contribute to the perpetuation of U.S. vulnerability to Russian missiles in deference to past deterrence practice? Is this not a dangerous balancing act? The inherent limitations of deterrence theory and practice would seem to argue for ending U.S. vulnerability to missiles from all sources, including Russian missiles.

The key to this seeming dilemma involves a pragmatic approach to the balancing act. Mutual U.S.-Russian vulnerability to missile attack clearly does carry a risk of mutual annihilation—the probability of which cannot be controlled fully or even known. We do not, for example, know the margin of error that should be attached to prognoses about stability. That margin probably is considerably smaller in U.S.-Russian relations given the history of the relationship. Nevertheless, grandiose claims to the contrary, no one knows how to ensure future deterrence stability even in U.S.-Russian relations. This, of course, is why leaders on both sides have identified exiting the mutual vulnerability deterrence relationship as a long-term goal. The issue here is the practical

---

demonstrably designed to address only rogue missile threats, and the U.S. agenda is, in fact, limited to meeting the limited proliferation threat. Moving beyond such limited NMD capabilities in a cooperative manner would necessitate a very dramatic improvement in political relations. See Keith Payne and Andrei Kortunov, *Proliferation and the Potential for Russian-American Cooperation* (forthcoming).

44. See for example Sergei Kortunov, "The Deterrent Forces of the Commonwealth of Independent States," in, *Nuclear Weapons in the Changing World*, Patrick Garrity and Steven Maaranen, ed. (New York: Plenum Press, 1992), 65–76. On the U.S. side, the Senate's START II Resolution of Ratification states: "The long-term perpetuation of deterrence based on mutual and severe offensive nuclear threats would be outdated in a strategic environment in which the United States and Russian Federation are seeking to put aside their past adversarial relationship and instead build a relationship based upon trust rather than fear." From, *Congressional Record*, 26 January 1996, S463.

difference between defending effectively against the rogues' limited missile potential and defending against a Russian major missile attack option involving the thousands of warheads that would remain in the Russian arsenal even following START II. The U.S. may, for some time and through its own efforts, be capable of providing effective defenses against the limited missile capabilities expected of the rogues. In contrast, given the likely technical and budgetary constraints facing U.S. defensive programs, exiting the condition of mutual societal vulnerability vis-à-vis the Russian Federation may, if at all feasible, require cooperation with Russia. Cooperation could be in terms of both coordinated defensive deployments and offensive force reductions. This, in fact, was the basis for the concept of a "cooperative defensive transition" as discussed in the mid-1980s.[45] Unilateral U.S. NMD efforts could sidetrack that cooperation if those efforts are viewed in Moscow as a solo U.S. escape from missile vulnerability intended to undermine Russian security.[46]

Preventing the emergence of U.S. vulnerability to rogue missiles should be considered essential given the limitations of deterrence theory and practice. Moving away from mutual vulnerability with the Russian Federation also is a reasonable goal for the long term. We should not allow unfounded Russian concerns about limited U.S. NMD to prevent us from defending ourselves against rogue missile threats when they emerge; neither should we unnecessarily provoke the Russians with ambitious NMD plans that would preclude the cooperation necessary for addressing mutual vulnerability in the long run. The balance noted by Harold Brown above must be struck if at all possible: because deterrence cannot provide reliable protection, we should not accept vulnerability when we need not. And we should work cooperatively toward ending vulnerability in the long term in that case where we may be unable to do so unilaterally given realistic defense budget limitations and possible technical constraints.

---

45. For an early elaboration of the "cooperative defensive transition" see Colin S. Gray, "Deterrence, Arms Control, and the Defense Transition," *Orbis* 28, no. 2 (Summer 1984): 227–40.

46. This is the leitmotiv of the Russian contribution to Payne and Kortunov, *Proliferation and the Potential for Russian-American Cooperation*.

The basic thesis of much Cold War thinking about deterrence in U.S.-Soviet relations was that mutual vulnerability was inescapable and that there was "literally no chance" for nuclear use because of the enormous potential costs of conflict and nuclear escalation. Deterrence stability in the U.S.-Soviet relationship thus was considered both sturdy and the best that was possible under the circumstances.

In a very articulate summary of this thesis, Professor Robert Jervis observes that:

> Because force cannot be easily controlled or compartmentalized, the fear of nuclear war does deter the other side from much more than nuclear attack. Irrational as it may be, the chance of devastation has made our world unusually safe.
>
> . . . As long as the societies of both sides are vulnerable (and few except President Reagan believe that missile defenses will ever be able to protect cities), gaining military advantage or denying it to the other side is much less important than the risks states are willing to run to further their values. . . . . The fact that neither side can protect itself without the other's cooperation drastically alters the way in which force can be used or threatened.
>
> I believe that each side's awareness of the utter destructiveness of large-scale nuclear war means that the chances of war between the United States and the USSR are very slight—even if the United States continues to follow it foolish policy [i.e., the "War-Fighting" approach]—and that the Russians can be deterred from major military adventures.[47]

There are two important propositions imbedded in this Cold War thesis: first, that mutual vulnerability is a condition of great safety because it is a basis for deterrence stability; and second, that vulnerability is inescapable "without the other's cooperation." In thinking about the future role of missile defense, however, it is

---

47. See *The Illogic of American Nuclear Strategy* (Ithaca, N.Y.: Cornell Univ. Press, 1984), 12-14.

critical that we question whether either proposition is likely to hold for U.S. relations with rogue states in the second nuclear age.

I have examined that first proposition about the high degree of safety that supposedly can be attributed to deterrence. The dubiousness of that proposition suggested here has implications for the second proposition concerning the certainty of vulnerability. Because the reliability of deterrence clearly appears to be questionable vis-à-vis the variety of rogue states that are self-described as hostile to the United States, denying them the capability to hold U.S. cities hostage to WMD threats and attack should be of foremost interest. Moving forward with effective missile defense in this regard, as now appears to be quite feasible,[48] would be a critical step in this effort.

Over time, denying rogues the capability to threaten U.S. cities with missiles armed with WMD may prove infeasible, as was thought to be the case vis-à-vis the Soviet Union during the Cold War. The differences in resources and technical prowess between the United States and rogues, however, may well be so great that we can postpone for many years, or even indefinitely, the emergence of the inescapable societal vulnerability to missile attack that was thought to characterize the Cold War and was a basic ingredient in Cold War thinking about deterrence.

Final Comment

For policies of deterrence in the second nuclear age, those important contextual factors largely dismissed by Assured Vulnerability

---

48. There appears to be a strong bipartisan consensus on the ready technical feasibility of defense against limited missile threats. For example, according to the Arms Control Association (no friend to missile defense), "There is little doubt that it is technically possible to protect the United States against a handful of missiles launched by accident, a mad commander, or a Third World country." The Arms Control Association, Background Paper, *New Star Wars Plan: Unnecessary Destruction of the ABM Treaty*, February 1991, 1. Secretary of Defense William Perry has rendered a similar technical judgment, stating that the defensive systems now in development "would be quite capable of defending against the much smaller and relatively unsophisticated ICBM threat that a rogue nation or a terrorist could mount any time in the foreseeable future." See Remarks Prepared for Delivery by William J. Perry, Secretary of Defense, George Washington University, 25 April 1996, News Release No. 241-96, Office of Assistant Secretary of Defense (Public Affairs), 26 April 1996, 4. William Graham, Science Advisor to Presidents Reagan and Bush, also concludes that effective defense against limited missile threats poses no technical problem for the United States. Cited in "Former Science Advisor Sees Bright Future for Missile Defense," *Defense Daily* (Special Supplement), 31 October 1991, S-1.

as serious possible sources of failure will have to be given their due place of prominence. In attempting to identify "how to deter" regional challengers, the initial question will be "How much do you know about the challenger?" The answer to this question, it is hoped, will provide an informed basis for answering the question, "How much [threat] is enough?"

During the Cold War, the Minimum Deterrence and MAD approaches to strategic deterrence policy attempted to answer this second question without addressing the first, largely on the basis of intuition or very simple assumptions about the opponent. Following a similar course in the second nuclear age—assuming that nuclear deterrence will work because the foe will be sensible by our standards—will not by any means provide the basis for a deterrence policy that can be considered "conclusive" or is "ensured" to work, whether nuclear weapons are part of the threat or not. The hubris of the Cold War in this regard will be dangerous because it falsely promises the reliability of deterrence policies. The key to creating the most reliable deterrence policies possible for the future will be intelligence. Even with substantial information on the challenger, however, deterrence policies will not be reliable in the sense typically promised by defense officials and commentators—we will not know how they will perform in any specific case until after the fact, if then.

Thus, in the absence of persuasive information to the contrary, we should hedge against the possibility that deterrence will fail. Policies of regional deterrence that exploit threats based on those U.S. military capabilities that would prove useful in the event deterrence fails will be most reasonable, that is, deterrence by denial. This approach is very different from much of the Cold War's strategic deterrence consideration or even NATO's Flexible Response policy; each ultimately rested on nuclear threats that could not be executed without grossly jeopardizing national survival. Even the so-called War-Fighting approach sought to prepare for the initial failure of deterrence only by adding more layers of deterrence to the equation—"intra-war deterrence." Preparing for catastrophic deterrence failure in the sense of preparing to limit damage to the U.S. homeland if a rogue challenger ultimately cannot be deterred and actually shoots at us would be a dramatic change from Assured Vulnerability thinking, which essentially was based on the view that such preparation was fruitless and destabilizing.

U.S. expeditionary forces are likely to be the mainstay of U.S. regional deterrence threats in the future, particularly as the United States continues to withdraw forward-deployed forces. If so, these forces need to be rapidly deployable to prevent challengers from anticipating the possibility of a fait accompli, and sufficiently awe-inspiring to impress even hardened challengers. Because conventional weapons are likely to be inadequately "fearsome" in some cases, as appears to have been demonstrated by Saddam Hussein's decision-making, the United States should retain nuclear threats for regional contingencies. They should not be placed in the background so definitively as appears to be the current intention of the United States, lest regional challengers begin to understand the degree to which the nuclear taboo shapes U.S. decision-making.

Finally, although stigmatized by the Assured Vulnerability paradigm, missile defense should receive a new lease on life in the second nuclear age. NMD and TMD may become increasingly essential, both for reasons of their prospective contribution to regional deterrence credibility and in preparation for deterrence failure. Missile defense may bolster our own regional deterrence capability and threat, undermine a regional challenger's capability to deter and coerce us, and provide protection when deterrence fails.

Chapter 6
Summary and Conclusion

In the midst of peace, war is looked upon as an object too distant to merit consideration.

—Vegetius, 390 A.D.

It would be difficult to overstate the degree to which the axioms of Assured Vulnerability have captured U.S. policy and thought regarding deterrence. In civilian and military seminars and studies, recognition occasionally is expressed of the need to rethink deterrence policy. Yet the basic assumptions of Assured Vulnerability remain largely unexamined and unchallenged: opponents are assumed to be subject to U.S. deterrence policies, to be rational, sensible, well-informed, and predictably cowed by severe U.S. threats. With several notable and welcome recent exceptions, expressions to this effect by officials and expert commentators are numerous and clear. Appreciation of the many mechanisms by which deterrence policies can fail—even when backed by nuclear threats—appears to be virtually absent except among a handful of academic specialists. An occasional reference to the possibility of rogue irrationality typically is followed by reassuring comments that nuclear weapons will continue to deter, particularly in the case of "established" nuclear powers. The problem, of course, is that deterrence policies can fail for a multitude of reasons beyond irrationality that do not appear to be so rare. Those reasons cannot be wholly checked with certainty even in U.S.-Russian relations. They are likely to be more prevalent in relations with rogues—the moral being that we can have little confidence at this point that nuclear weapons will deter reliably and predictably.

Acceptance of Assured Vulnerability has been bipartisan, as is the reluctance to question its applicability to the second nuclear age. This reluctance is as evident in military discussions as in civilian. During the Cold War, political conservatives typically favored the War-Fighting approach to nuclear deterrence policies, while liberals embraced some form of Minimum Deterrence or

MAD. Yet, all were captives of the Assured Vulnerability deterrence framework. That framework will not provide predictably useful guidance for the second nuclear age, particularly vis-à-vis rogues and terrorists.

Nevertheless, deterrence is too valuable a tool to adopt a defeatist attitude. Sun Tzu undoubtedly was correct in identifying the successful use of threats for deterrence and coercion as the "acme of skill." Effective deterrence polices are extremely advantageous, preventing provocations before they occur and eliminating the need to wage war to force a challenger to behave properly. U.S. policies of nuclear deterrence probably played an important role in moderating Soviet behavior during the Cold War, although it is difficult to prove the proposition in any definitive sense. And effective policies of deterrence will be needed for the second nuclear age, as regional challengers, undisciplined by the Cold War blocs, emerge armed with WMD and missiles. As noted earlier, Secretary of Defense William Perry rightly observed in 1991 that, "The United States does not want to spend the rest of the decade fighting regional conflicts. The key to avoiding such entanglements is to use its new strength to deter these conflicts rather than fight them."[1]

Nevertheless, in the absence of "knowing the opponent" and tailoring deterrence policies to fit the specific case, regional deterrence in the second nuclear age will be too unpredictable for us to assume its effectiveness. Even when information about the challenger is available and efforts are made to tailor deterrence to the occasion, its effectiveness will not be "ensured" or "conclusive." U.S. leaders, in sharp contrast to past practice, will need to take seriously the potential for deterrence failure. This potential will likely be considerably more pronounced in U.S. relations with regional rogues, but it is an irreducible risk in any attempt to translate deterrence theory into deterrence policy. Repeated claims by senior officials and commentators to the contrary, in the absence of substantial intelligence and "tailoring," confident promises

---

1. William J. Perry, "Desert Storm and Deterrence," *Foreign Affairs* 70, no. 4 (fall 1991): 82.

about deterrence working predictably should be recognized as hubris.

Deterrence theory can explain how leaders *should* behave, assuming the challenger's rationality and a variety of additional contextual conditions. Deterrence policies, however, cannot provide the basis for confident prediction about how a particular challenger *will* behave because of the stark gap separating deterrence theory assumptions concerning decision-making and the manner in which leaders sometimes actually make decisions. The now-traditional deterrence framework of the Cold War discounted the various factors that can degrade rational and well in formed decision-making, including the potential for ignorance, miscalculation, misjudgment, and irrationality. Yet, historical case studies typically demonstrate that such factors can and in fact have affected decision-making, particularly under conditions of crisis and stress.

This does not imply that deterrence theory lacks consistency or value. Rather, it may simply be deficient with regard to a particular context. It should not be expected to be a useful basis for establishing reliable deterrence policies when rationality, mutual familiarity, communication, and so forth, are inadequate. The difficulty for U.S. leaders in the second nuclear age will be in having sufficient information about the challenger to distinguish between those cases where the conditions for deterrence working pertain and those when they do not. Acquiring substantial information about the challenger should be helpful in this regard. In principle, the more that is known about the factors determining the challenger's decision-making, the more effective should be U.S. deterrence policies. Assuming a generically sensible foe will present considerable risk. In contrast to past practice, deterrence goals of the second nuclear age will require devoting at least as much attention to the question "How much do you know?" of the opponent as to the traditional question "How much is enough?"

Unfortunately, acquiring a database suitable to inform deterrence policies may be very difficult, involving a potentially very diverse set of opaque factors that could drive a challenger's decision-making. This difficulty is one of the reasons why deterrence analyses of the past have made simple assumptions about these important contextual factors and have proceeded to analyze that piece of the puzzle most amenable to precise calculation: the military balance. This was akin to looking for lost car keys only where the light happened to be good. But simply because knowing the challenger in useful ways may be difficult does not justify assuming a generically sensible and well informed foe. Such an assumption can easily be misleading, guiding the creation of deterrence policies as likely to provoke as to deter, as was the case in U.S.-Japanese relations in 1941.

In the second nuclear age, our familiarity with various regional challengers is likely to be more limited than it was with the Soviet Union during the Cold War. And we shall have to focus our attention on multiple potential challengers. They will be more likely to behave in ways not anticipated by U.S. leaders, and reliable, predictable deterrence policies will be farther from reach. This apprehension about deterrence policies based on the assumption of a generically sensible foe, as opposed to detailed contextual knowledge, is a far cry from the Assured Vulnerability approach, which tended to treat deterrence as an exercise in deductive logic about "country A" and "country B." It also is a direct challenge to those continuing definitive and blanket assurances voiced by senior officials and commentators about nuclear deterrence working against rogues as it purportedly did against the Soviet Union during the Cold War.

Regional deterrence policies in the second nuclear age should, of course, be made as sturdy as possible. This may be quite difficult in some cases, such as when U.S. capabilities will be called on to "deter the deterrent" of a desperate challenger. Such a goal may be more difficult than any challenge undertaken by U.S. Cold War policies. In addition, U.S. regional policies should take into account the potential for deterrence failure or irrelevance, in the sense of being prepared to frustrate the challenger's military goals and directly enforce U.S. will. Preparation for deterrence failure suggests the need to move toward "deterrence by denial," recognizing that the forces supporting regional deterrence threats should not be too far removed from the forces that actually would prove militarily useful. This also is a change, of course, from Assured Vulnerability, which was built on the notion that a useful level of societal protection would be infeasible if deterrence failed catastrophically.

Given the retraction of U.S. forward-based forces, conventional and nuclear, U.S. regional deterrence policies of the second nuclear age may of necessity be based on force projection capabilities. Fortunately, these capabilities may simultaneously serve the purpose of preparing for deterrence failure. Unless information about the challenger indicates otherwise, deterrence by denial will be the name of the game in the second nuclear age.

In addition, because of the potential difficulties of establishing credible deterrence threats and the possibility of confronting highly motivated challengers, nuclear threats should not be abandoned for regional deterrence duties. The U.S. drive to sweep them into the background for nonproliferation purposes should be moderated by their potential importance for deterrence, as again was demonstrated during the Gulf war. Nuclear threats cannot ensure that our deterrence policies will be conclusive, but on occasion they may make the difference between success and failure. The number of nuclear weapons helpful for regional deterrence missions probably is relatively small (rogue states simply have far fewer targets of any type than did the Soviet Union). But rogue leaders will have to believe that the possibility for U.S. nuclear use is real. In this regard, perceptions of U.S. determination and the types of nuclear weapons available may be key. There is ample and fertile ground here for informed psychological operations.

Finally, the second nuclear age places missile defense in a very different context from that of the Cold War, when conventional wisdom in the United States was that missile defense was infeasible, unnecessary, or destabilizing. In the future, missile defenses may be key both to preparation for deterrence failure and to the credibility of U.S. threats to project force against challengers armed with WMD. If the capability to "deter their deterrent" is suspect, then the capability to protect against rogue missile threats will be critical.

Most of the above recommendations flowing from this assessment of deterrence in the second nuclear age represent a dramatic shift away from the Assured Vulnerability paradigm. Such a shift will not be popular or come easily. There has been too much intellectual and policy investment in Assured Vulnerability for it to fall gently from its place of prominence—as demonstrated by the continuing confident statements from U.S. officials and commentators that are its reflection. Assured Vulnerability represents the basis for the bipartisan arms control and deterrence policy priesthood to claim special knowledge and to make relatively easy predictions about deterrence "stability." In its absence, commenting on "how to deter" becomes a messy process once again, requiring the difficult task of determining how much we know about a particular challenger.

The reception has not been—and will not be—warm for those who are skeptical of Assured Vulnerability and the confidence derived from it and who seriously question its applicability for the second nuclear age. Nevertheless, to mount such a challenge could prove important in terms of people's lives and the expenditure of resources. It is hoped that this book will serve as a helpful step forward.

Index

missiles, 18–20, 22–24, 25–29, 31,
34, 41, 43, 50, 82, 109, 121, 143–
148, 150, 152, 156; missile
attack, 22, 43, 59, 134, 145, 147,
149–150, 152; proliferation of,
xii, 18–20, 22, 143, 146; threat,
18, 23, 25, 145, 147, 149–150,
159; strike, 81, 143. *See also* MX
missile; Scud missile
Miyazawa, Kiichi, 20
Molotov–Ribbentrop pact, 114
Mongols, 97
morale, 24
motivation, 79, 91, 94, 108–110,
112–113, 115–117, 123, 125, 129
multipolar, 147
Munich, 53
Muto, Kabun, 21–22
mutual assured destruction (MAD),
7, 58, 61–71, 101, 127, 130, 147,
153, 156
mutual deterrence, 98–99
mutual sufficiency, 65
mutual vulnerability, 65, 149–151
MX missile, xi, 50

national missile defense (NMD),
142–143, 147–148, 150, 154
national security, ix, 52, 59;
national security strategy, x, 4–
5, 72
National Security Council, 139
New York Times, 48
Nicholas I, Tsar, 106
Nicholas II, Tsar, 112–113
1994 Nuclear Posture Review, 15
Nodong-1, 18, 27
nonproliferation, xii, 138, 145–147,
159
North Africa, 18–19
North America, 142
North Atlantic Treaty Organization
(NATO), xi, 20, 32–34, 125, 153;
1991 Rome Summit, 20; 1994
Brussels Summit, 20
North Korea, xii, 17–22, 27, 34, 57–
59, 79, 103, 107, 131 139, 143
nuclear age, 1, 9, 66, 97–98, 105
nuclear attack, 42, 44, 59, 79, 151

nuclear balance, 50–52
nuclear capabilities, U.S., 64–65, 67
nuclear debate, xi, 1, 8
nuclear deterrence, ix, 6–7, 15, 37–
41, 43–44, 46, 48, 52–53, 72, 80,
85, 87, 94, 98, 122, 137–138,
155–156, 158
nuclear forces, 8, 64, 67–69, 72, 93,
131, 139
nuclear freeze, xi, 8, 47
nuclear modernization, 7, 47
Nuclear Nonproliferation Treaty
(NPT), 138
nuclear posture, 15, 44
nuclear powers, 59
nuclear strategy, 65, 67
nuclear survivability, 42
nuclear threat, 1, 6, 30, 32, 42, 44,
48, 61–63, 65–66, 69–73, 80, 82–
84, 87, 92, 96–97, 99, 117, 119,
121–122, 128–131, 136, 137,
140, 142, 153–155, 159
nuclear umbrella, U.S., 17, 20
nuclear use, 6, 26, 29–31, 43, 47–48,
67, 70, 85, 137–140, 142, 151,
159; taboo against, 137–140, 154
nuclear war, ix, 5–6, 32, 49, 50, 98
nuclear weapons, 1, 5–7, 22, 26, 28–
30, 39, 44–45, 49, 58, 64, 70, 76,
80–81, 84–85, 96, 99–100, 101,
117, 121, 128, 136–139, 141,
147, 155, 159; development, 12,
17, 20, 139
Nunn, Sam, 76
Nye, Joseph, 41, 44

O'Neill, Robert, 116
On the Origins of War, 77, 79

Palestine, 29; Palestine Liberation
Front, 28
Panama, 11
Park Young-su, 143
Patriot missile, 143–145
peace, x, 29, 50–51, 77, 94, 99–100,
110, 155
Pearl Harbor, 55, 109–111
Pentagon, 15, 42
Perry, William, 13, 44, 58–59, 101,